SHE READS TRUTH

978-1-4336-8898-0

Published by B&H Publishing Group
Nashville, Tennessee

Authors are represented by Alive Literary Agency, 7680 Goddard
Street, Colorado Springs, Colorado, 80920, www.aliveliterary.com.

Cover Text Illustration: Cymone Wilder
Cover Design: Amanda Barnhart
Interior Design: Amanda Barnhart

Dewey Decimal Classification: 248.843
Subject Heading: WOMEN / FAITH / CHRISTIAN LIFE

2 3 4 5 6 7 8 • 22 21 20 19 18

SHE READS TRUTH

Holding Tight to Permanent
in a World That's Passing Away

RAECHEL MYERS &
AMANDA BIBLE WILLIAMS

PUBLISHING GROUP
NASHVILLE, TENNESSEE

To the "Shes" who read Truth:
Read on.

She Reads Truth was a community long before it was a book.

In 2012, a handful of strangers began reading God's Word together every day, staying connected with the hashtag #SheReadsTruth. This hashtag gave way to a website, which gave way to an app, and the movement continues to grow. Today, hundreds of thousands of women gather online to open our Bibles together and find Jesus there.

This community of "Women in the Word of God every day" represents a long list of cities and countries, a variety of backgrounds and traditions. We are women of all ages and life phases, with our own joys and sorrows and hopes, our own real-life stories. But there is a commonality that binds us: we believe God's Word is Truth. So we read.

Every day we read a new passage together—working our way through books of the Bible, topics that matter, and seasons of the Church calendar. We engage with God's Word and with each other. And we keep coming back, on the hard days and the good days, because God and His Word never change, regardless of our circumstances.

We invite you to read along with us at shereadstruth.com or on the She Reads Truth app.

A NOTE TO THE READER

This book was written by two people. In fact, a good portion of the chapters alternate between two separate memoirs. Because both of our stories are stretched across the pages of this book, we've indicated the author at the beginning of each chapter. Our stories are different, but that's the point. The Truth is the same in both of them. It's the Truth in your story too.

CONTENTS

PASSING AWAY

S ix months to a year, Day Three."

I spoke into my phone as I rounded the corner at 17th and Holly and drove past the large ivory house with the matching scalloped fence.

That house had been a favorite of mine since we moved up the street to a different corner, eight years prior. I loved it for the wraparound porch and the full-sized bedframe they'd fashioned into a porch swing. I loved it for its tall windows and that lovely fence. And I loved it for the big tree in the corner of the yard, the tree whose leaves were fading to yellow on that October afternoon.

It was there, driving past the big ivory house, that the thought first occurred to me: my father is fading like the leaves on that tree.

I'd started leaving voice memos on my phone the day my dad was given his most devastating diagnosis to date—stage four esophageal cancer. They'd do chemotherapy in an effort to put off the inevitable, but the disease would prevail and a year was our best-case scenario.

I recorded these messages to myself to mark the days, speaking into my phone while driving to the hospital or doing dishes or watching my twin baby boys eat breakfast in their matching high chairs. When I play the messages back I can hear their small voices in the background, another reminder of how quickly things change.

Life is a given until it isn't.

Death is so much easier to ignore when it's an abstract concept, one newscast removed. Death on a timer, however, demands constant attention. For my family in those long months, dying, not living, was our new sure thing.

My father was seventy-four when he passed away just four years ago—recently enough that when I think of him, the memories of him slipping away are brighter than the decades that came before. Those years will come back too, I think, but right now they are faded and black and white. The passing away is all I can see in vivid color.

It's strange the things our minds and hearts choose to keep near the surface, memories at the ready. Here are the things I remember from the thirty-three years before the dying started, in no particular order:

I remember Fourth of July fireworks in our driveway when I was small, with friends-turned-family from the neighborhood where I grew up. Our house sat at the top of the hill and everyone would trek up with their lawn chairs and a contribution to the show of sparks and smoke. The helicopters were my favorite.

I remember the sound of his voice, the voice the cancer eventually took.

I remember him working—always working. He was a golf professional since before I was born, and I have image after image of him in my mind, standing behind the counters of the various golf courses he ran over the years, greeting the golfers as they signed in and keeping a close eye on the cart return. I can see him on the tractor, mowing the greens at dusk.

I remember the baggy overalls I wore in high school that he hated, a fact he only said out loud once but somehow I would never forget. I remember how he combed his hair just so, no matter the day or the occasion.

I remember the way he smiled at me and my husband as we danced on our wedding day, and how the approval I saw in that smile made my heart so proud and relieved.

Everything else, almost every big and little thing, is a blur. It's unsettling, isn't it? How can thirty years be reduced to a glass not even half full?

But those last three years—they make me smile through my tears. They are the brightest though they were the darkest, the happiest though heavy with sorrow. And I see it all as clear as if it were happening in live action on a screen in front of me.

At the time, I would have likened our real-life drama to a tragedy, equal parts suspense and sorrow. But looking back, I believe it was more of an adventure, though not the kind a person seeks. We were precariously perched on a mountain with no way down and nothing to do but keep climbing.

When you're in that place—clinging to the side of a wall made of rock, a storm of uncontrollable circumstances swirling around you—what you're holding on to becomes clear. Place your foot on shale, and it will crumble beneath you. Grab hold of a loose ledge, and your hand will slip. But hold tight to the mountain itself, and it will hold you up.

The firm handholds along the journey of my dad's illness included these:

> "I have told you these things so that in Me you may have peace. You will have suffering in this world. Be courageous! I have conquered the world." (John 16:33)

Do you not know? Have you not heard? Yahweh is the everlasting God, the Creator of the whole earth. He never grows faint or weary; there is no limit to His understanding. (Isa. 40:28)

I remain confident of this: I will see the goodness of the LORD in the land of the living. (Ps. 27:13 NIV)

"And remember, I am with you always, to the end of the age." (Matt. 28:20)

The promises themselves were true, and we held on tight. But their immutability was inseparable from the Promiser. These rocks of promise are part of the steadfast mountain of God's covenant. His Word is true because He Himself is true (Heb. 13:8).

When everything around us was withering and fading away, my father included, God and His Word stood firm (Isa. 40:8).

The hospital was a time warp with sterile floors and familiar faces. My mom and brother and I spent our hours going to and from the intensive-care unit on a special elevator, with breaks in the cafeteria where we could get an Internet signal and a sandwich.

Sacred moments would arrive unexpectedly. A visit to the hospital chapel while a pianist played music on the baby grand in the hall. Spontaneous tears and hugs in the middle of a busy hallway. The time a stranger stopped to console me on a bench near the parking garage, embracing me like the ambassador of Christ she was. But the most sacred moments were always there in the hospital room with him, reluctantly but earnestly acting out the final scenes from his life's play to a score of beeping machines and the ventilator's steady sigh.

Those days are some of my most treasured times with my father.

He couldn't speak, so we used whatever paper was handy to write our conversations in fragmented pieces. And any time a precious stretch of days or weeks arrived where he was well enough to be at home, it was like being on vacation.

My dad would sit in the red chair in our living room and watch his grandchildren play, laughing at their antics, his eyes keeping pace with their active little legs. They'd crawl up into his lap, being careful to avoid the tube in his stomach and the oxygen attached to his throat. He'd flip through board books with them, sit contentedly while they ran Matchbox cars up and down the arms of his chair, and pretend to bite their toddler-boy fingers, scrunching his nose into a smile as they laughed. I had never seen my dad's sun-weathered face any happier than in these rare moments of reprieve in his final months.

Though he never said it aloud—he couldn't—I knew what this was. My father was looking up; he was looking around. His whole life he held fast, head down, to the foothold of hard work, anchoring himself firmly to the noble goal of providing for his family. But, as humans are prone to do, he focused so intently on that single foothold for so long, he lost sight of the mountain itself, the reasons the foothold mattered to begin with.

Meanwhile, my mother and brother and I gripped onto our footholds. The goodness of the Lord in the land of the living. Like the psalmist, we were watching for it. We were waiting.

We gripped that promise with one hand while doing what we could to care for my father with the other. We arrived at the ICU early each morning for shift change, asking about the last night's stats and the testing and treatment plans for the day. We called the nurse at midnight and 3 a.m. to make sure he was resting and his oxygen levels weren't falling. We silenced the beeping when the IV bags ran dry, adjusted his pillows, and kept his feet warm with those hospital gripper socks that have the smiley faces on the bottom. But no matter what we did, there was no taking this suffering away—not Dad's and not ours.

The apostle Paul warned us about this in his letter to the new believers at Corinth. Love—the love that is the essence of our God and His Son, our Savior—will last. But nothing else on earth will. "Love never ends. As for prophecies, *they will pass away*; as for tongues, *they will cease*; as for knowledge, *it will pass away*. For we know in part and we prophesy in part, but *when the perfect comes, the partial will pass away*" (1 Cor. 13:8–10 ESV, emphasis mine).

In my daily, right-now life, I've become a professional death-avoider. I close my eyes and ears when the news of the world's pain becomes too heavy. I avoid eye contact with the man who's heaped his worldly belongings on a sidewalk grate downtown. And I certainly don't visit the ICU waiting room in my free time.

It's easier to focus my efforts on crafting something solid than it is to acknowledge that this temporary world is passing away just like the leaves of that fading tree at 17th and Holly. Still, when I try to force permanence where there is none, I am always disappointed. We cannot know the eternal weight of this temporary life we've been given unless we understand that it is, indeed, temporary. Paul knew this about us too.

"For now we see in a mirror dimly, but then face to face. Now I know in part; then I shall know fully, even as I have been fully known" (1 Cor. 13:12 ESV). There is a reason the shift in my father's gaze mattered, and there is a reason that promise from Psalms held true. The handhold did not hold because of our determined, white-knuckled grip. The things we cling to can be good and true, but only because they are part of something much greater and truer than the world can offer: the immovable mountain of God's eternal Truth.

God's Word is more than a foothold, more than a verse to chant when life's foundations are crumbling and you're trying like mad to caulk the cracks. God's Word itself, in the first verse of that very same hospital psalm, says that God is our stronghold—a place to hide, a place to dwell, a place to be safe.

The gospel of Jesus Christ is not a rock we stand on to climb a mountain; it is the Rock, the Mountain. It is His faithfulness that holds me, not mine that holds Him. The footholds only hold because they are part of the Rock of Ages.

On a Monday morning in June, eight months after that first voice memo, my dad left this temporary world with its temporary joys and sorrows. And while it was the deepest pain I've ever known, I have never had a greater honor than being there at his side, watching Rex Bible pass through to the place where he now sees face-to-face.

It was not Psalm 27 that kept care of my family while we watched my father die. In fact, none of those verses we whispered ushered my father into Glory. It was God Himself, the Perfect One—the whole of His Truth and His covenant to us as His people—that covered us when we were hanging on the side of the mountain, just trying to weather the storm without losing our grip.

This world is still passing away, just like my dad did, just like autumn leaves do and like you and I will. But God and His Word will never pass away (Matt. 24:35). He is the one permanent thing we find when we frantically grasp in the dark of our doubt and fear. He is the perfection we long for in the midst of our suffering and brokenness. He is the one sure thing we seek in our uncertainty.

God is our only immovable mountain, and we can find Him in His Word.

SHE IS ME

She is me.
She is you.
She wants faith, hope, and love.
She wants help and healing.
She wants to hear and be heard, to see and be seen.
She wants things set right.

She wants to know what is true—not partly true, or sometimes true, or almost true. She wants to see Truth itself, face-to-face.

But here, now, these things are all cloudy. Hope is tinged with hurt. Faith is shaded by doubt. Lesser, broken things masquerade as love.

Real love is the God who became flesh—a living, feeling human being. He is God with us, rescuing the dying, calling the sinners, and embracing those who are wasting away. Real hope is the God who came to set things right. He came to set the cloudy mirror aside for good so we can see Him, face-to-face. Real Truth is the Word that created the world, the Truth that never ceases to be true. Counterfeits no longer interest her; she is looking for the realest thing. This is why she reads.

She reads Truth to find Jesus.

And He is there, on every page, greater than her triumphs and shame, vaster than her needs and her pain. Those are real, to be certain. But they are the partial, the passing away. Jesus—and Jesus alone—is the Perfect, the Permanent.

The Truth does not magically erase her suffering or cure her disappointment. It does not negate her struggle or invalidate her sorrow. It does something even better—it leads her into relationship with the One who made her and makes her new, the One who is greater than all of these. The Truth brings her face-to-face with the God who has never stopped loving His children, who has never failed to do what He says He will do. The Truth is love in black and white—a love that does not change, even when her Bible is closed.

One day the cloudy mirror will be gone. One day face-to-face is the only way she will see.

Until then, she reads Truth—not just for answers or equations, help or how-tos. She reads Truth to find the perfect and permanent One. She reads Truth because she needs Jesus.

WHAT'S IN YOUR CUP?

Holding Tight to Permanent
in a World That's Passing Away

L ife began with a big sister, canning tomatoes, snapping beans, and learning to pump on the tall swings at the park down the street. Oversized lilac trees and grapevines grew wild in the backyard of our small-town Victorian, and the chipping paint on the wraparound porch provided endless satisfaction for busy little hands on long summer evenings. There were bicycle rides into town and the wounded bird we nursed back to flight and the giant mounds of construction dirt we slid down until my sister cut her foot and the fun was over for that day.

The little years were sweet ones. Uncomplicated. True.

When I was in kindergarten, our black lab Daisy would sometimes show up at recess to chase the girls and nip at the boys and when the bell rang to come in, she'd race home with some hat or scarf treasure I'd always have to surrender to my teacher at school the next day.

That was four, five, and six. A things-will-never-change world of walking to school, pints of white milk, pigtails and suntanned shoulders, and finally becoming a member of The Hundreds Club. Fireflies were my "yeses" and learning to ride a two-wheeler was my "amen."

Then came the Barbie wedding.

We'd been planning it for a week with our babysitter, Megan. My sister and I in our nightgowns and bedheads skipped breakfast in favor of picking just the right bridesmaid dress for Skipper. It was an important day, and everything was going to be just perfect. But before Megan could arrive, the phone rang. Dad's neck was broken. Another motorcycle accident. The Barbie wedding would have to happen another day.

It was right around then that our things-will-never-change world turned upside down for good. Dad's neck recovered, but the crash was a symptom of something much bigger. His self-medicated manic episodes caused by bipolar disorder were beginning to not only motivate reckless behavior (like racing motorcycles sitting backwards across train tracks), but he was becoming a danger to his family as well.

I remember watching confused and scared through the railing of the stairs as my mama endured the yelling and being flung across the room. I remember being picked up from kindergarten, loaded onto a motorcycle without a helmet, and riding a state away to check on the eggs in the nest at a rest stop we found a week earlier, or to visit an arcade six towns over. Endless tokens and soda and mechanical animals would rule my Tuesday evening into the night. Some nights, I would be awakened from a deep sleep to my dad telling me to get into the car, then driving to the grocery store to buy cigarettes and candy bars. I'd be tucked back into bed with a whisper of "don't tell anyone." We called them our "midnight rides."

By the time I was seven, the self-medicated mania became too much for my mother. The drugs within reach of children. The impulsive behavior. The yelling. So much yelling.

One first-grade afternoon, my mom picked us up from school. Instead of driving home, and without notice, we turned onto the gravel driveway of an empty house about a mile out of town. There we sat, engine still running, backpacks still on our backs, and our mom told us the thing I'll never forget.

I sat motionless in the backseat of the car, afraid movement would be taken as a reaction and I had no idea how to react. My eyes darted to my big sister seated next to me for clues. *What does separated mean? Is this exciting or sad? Why is the back of the station wagon full of our things? Where are we going to sleep tonight?*

That night we moved to a new town. That Sunday, a new church. That year, a new school. Everything was new. Temporary. Nothing was sure. Over the course of the next year we would sleep on a dozen different floors, on cots in the unfinished basements of classmates, then eventually we would move our cots to a one-bedroom apartment above the Main Street pub and the crisis pregnancy center. The thin walls were ineffective to quiet the arguments in the adjacent apartment. There was so much yelling.

Even though I didn't know how to express it then, I knew something was wrong about the life we'd left behind. But to a six-year-old, all-night arcade adventures fueled by Dr. Pepper and midnight motorcycle rides would always feel better than sleeping on cots in strange places. I didn't know which life I wanted more, but I soon understood I didn't have that choice. This was our new true. For a long time, nothing was certain except that life was uncertain.

FIGHTING FOR PERMANENT

We all have the same story, don't we? At least in some sense.

I may have gone first, but any one of you could go next and share in hesitant or colorful detail the moment you stood shattered as the most permanent thing in your life passed away before your eyes.

Maybe you didn't have a father with bipolar disorder and a drug abuse problem. But maybe someone you trusted very much hurt you very deeply. Or maybe your family packed up and moved away from the only home and friends you ever knew. Maybe this passing away was a physical death—a constant figure in your life whose slow or sudden death made you question the steadfastness of everything around you.

It's that first time, though, isn't it? That very first experience of our sureness undone. It shapes us forever.

I'll never forget my grandma Marvolene taking me out for lunch when I was a kid, quoting Ernestine Ulmer and winking as she leaned across the table and pointed to my menu, "Life is uncertain. Eat dessert first." I was terrified and exhilarated all at once at the sudden realization of all the uncertainties life held. Anything could happen! On the other hand, *anything* could happen.

By the time we're adults (and for some of us, even sooner), we understand that nothing will last forever. People change, seasons change, and the best and worst circumstances always eventually pass away.

This knowledge drives some of us to hold life loosely, kissing moments as they come, knowing they'll be gone before we know it. Others of us determine to manage our realities with a tight grip and an inflexible resolve. We record our lives with photographs and journals, not wanting a moment to pass without documenting, lest we forget it even happened.

Still some of us know all too well the pain of things passing, so we choose not to savor, not to record, and not to remember. We don't let people in because they will most certainly leave us, we don't take risks because something will absolutely go wrong, and we don't dare dream because dreaming leads to disappointment.

Whether we hold life loosely, with a tight grip, or at arm's length, adulthood has made every one of us keenly aware of how temporary life is. And to one degree or another, whether we like to admit it or not, we're all fighting for permanent.

Why do you think that is? What do we hope to find on the other side of permanent? And how do we hold tight to it once we've found it?

SAND AND STARS

A lot of men and women in the Bible were fighting for permanent just like us. And in most cases, their permanent passed away just as quickly.

Job's story is an obvious example of big life changes in a short time period, but the loss of his wealth and family is particularly dramatic. Job wasn't the only one. The same happened with Adam and Eve when they were sent out of the actual paradise of Eden into a newly fallen world. In Job's case, his loss was because of his righteousness, and in Adam and Eve's case, it was because of their disobedience. But they both lost their permanent in the blink of an eye.

Joseph was sold into slavery by his brothers one afternoon, later thrown into prison because Potiphar's wife lied, and he was eventually elevated from prisoner to King's assistant overnight. Permanent was not a theme in Joseph's life, but God's favor absolutely was.

Dramatic life changes aren't exclusively an Old Testament theme. Think of the lame man by the pools of Bethesda. When Jesus healed him, he left behind the life of a crippled beggar he'd known for thirty-eight years. Mary and Martha suffered the loss and celebrated the resurrection of their brother Lazarus, all in a matter of a couple of days. Saul encountered God on the road to Damascus and went from being a chief persecutor of Christians, to temporary blindness, to being an impassioned apostle of Jesus, with a new name.

And what about the disciples? They were all minding their own business when Jesus called them to drop everything and follow Him. Fast-forward a couple years and they're dining at the Last Supper with Jesus, with nothing close to a clear understanding of what the next three days would hold. Life would never be the same for any of them.

Life changes in an instant. But even when that change is unwelcome, we can give thanks because God is good.

Take Abraham, for example.

Abram's permanent was his family's land and his wife, Sarai. (Later they would be known as Abraham and Sarah. Not even names are permanent!)

Sarai's permanent was that she was barren. This was life as they had known it for all of their married life. At the ages of seventy-five and sixty-five, a barren couple was their reality. Together they lived in the land of Ur and had a family lineage that included worshiping false gods (Josh. 24:2–3).

Well. With God, it turns out that you're never too old for your circumstances to change, not even worshiping false gods or staying in the only country you've ever known. God came to Abram and said, "Go from your country, your people and your father's household to the land I will show you" (Gen. 12:1 NIV). Just like that, their permanent passed away forever. Life would never be the same.

The land in which they lived and the God they worshiped weren't the only circumstances that changed. It turns out that barrenness in your nineties is not even a permanent situation when God ordains something else. God promised Abram and Sarai a son. Not just a son, but descendants so numerous, they would outnumber the stars in the heavens and the sand in the sea.

If you're keeping track, that's us, you guys. We're the sand and the stars. (And if I get to pick, I would like to be a star.)

God's promise to Abram (known to theologians and 1 in 100 pedestrians as the Abrahamic Covenant) meant He was going to make him the father of a great nation. God would bless Abraham (there's that name change!), make his name great, curse anyone who curses him, and "all the peoples on earth will be blessed through [him]" (Gen. 12:2–3). This one-time, never-broken promise began the history of the people of Israel.

From Abraham and Sarah's small-picture view, leaving their home country and trusting the call of a God they barely knew must have been a tough moment. In fact, the Bible tells us that they were zoomed in tight on the details of how they would possibly conceive in their old age and how they would know where they were going and who to take with them.

But from God's whole-picture view, these complicated roadblocks were simply minor details. This was the beginning of a nation and a promise of faithfulness that would be kept and honored forever. It was a great blessing. In His goodness, God helped Abraham and Sarah take their eyes away from the lens of the telescope of their present circumstances to see the entire sky of stars, saying, "Look toward heaven, and number the stars, if you are able to number them. . . . So shall your offspring be" (Gen. 15:5 ESV). Not just one son, but an entire sky's worth of sons and daughters.

There would be more to Abraham's story than he could ever imagine.

BLUE EYES

There's more to my story, too.

We left seven-year-old Raechel in a station wagon somewhere between Life A and Life B. And from the looks of things, I was either at the end of something terrible or the beginning of something unknown. But the

15

truth is, it was neither. It was a continuation. Something great—something that was set into motion before I took my first breath—had always been underway. My small world was crumbling in chaos all around me, but all along, something bigger was happening. The rubble around First Grade Me was only proof that God was at work on a larger scale than I would ever fully understand.

One of the sweetest, most redeeming parts of my whole life story comes next.

My family fell apart after school on a Wednesday afternoon. That Sunday, in a new town, I woke up in a sleeping bag on a stranger's floor. My mom, sister, and I went to a new church. And even though I hadn't exactly met Jesus yet, this was the day I met my Boaz. My lowercase-r redeemer in more than a lot of ways.

I can't bring to memory much about that Sunday morning. I remember the first-grade Sunday school room with tables pushed together and metal folding chairs around them in the musty basement of an old, new-to-me, church. I remember our very tall teacher and his small, kind wife and the salt-and-pepper hair on both of their heads. They tried their best to keep a room full of enthusiastic seven-year-olds quiet. Most of all, I remember the wild blue eyes and curly blonde hair of the most unruly little boy I'd ever seen. He was the ringleader of the noisy bunch, and he fascinated me.

That image of Blue Eyes standing on his chair and waving his arms in excitement over who-knows-what will forever be burned in my memory as the moment I met my future husband. Of course, I didn't know it at the time. I probably thought I was meeting my nemesis. Everything I loved about order was the opposite of him. He was loud, and I felt quiet. Everyone was looking at him, and I'm not sure anyone even noticed me. I didn't know it that seven-year-old Sunday morning, but Blue Eyes would never stop being a part of my life from that moment on.

There is truth (our present circumstance), and there is truer Truth (the history of God's unwavering, faithful, covenant relationship with His people). Call it the "grand scheme of things" if you like, but I believe we make a big mistake when we trust God based only on what He's done for us today, or even in our own lifetime.

If a telescope zooms our gaze in on one particular thing, God's Word is like a wide-angle lens that shouts, "Remember! God is THIS BIG! He is a God of the big-picture!" When we're busy dialing in on legitimately important things like jobs and health and deadlines, it can do us a lot of good to remember what God did at creation, and what He promised Abraham. Remember how He kept His hand on Joseph, bringing Israel into Egypt and eventual slavery, then delivering them from slavery at the hand of Moses. All the while He promised on every page that an even bigger plan was unfolding!

This is what the Bible does. This is why we read Truth.

It's okay to study God's hand in our present circumstances. It's good and appropriate to move that telescope around to see what other people are dealing with too. But opening God's Word and studying His character is like lifting our eyes from the viewfinder long enough to remember that the God who calls us His people has been hanging the stars in the heavens since time began. Just as He was faithful then, He will be faithful now.

A PEEK AT REDEMPTION

Thirteen years after I met Ryan "Blue Eyes" Myers, I married him. (We were twenty-year-old babies when we got married. I'll get to that later.)

It still blows my mind to think that the wild-eyed little boy I met twenty-six years ago, the very week my family fell apart, would become the man who would ask for my hand and give me his name. God would use Ryan to show me what a husband can be, what a dad should be, and what a steady, loving presence really is. This friendship-turned-romance would continue to point me to Christ.

I told you he was my Boaz—a kinsman redeemer who God used to show me how all of the broken things in my family could look if they were made just a little more whole. Here's a brief recap of Boaz in the Bible. Ruth's relationship status went from married, to widowed, to near-homeless companion of her mother-in-law Naomi. And like Boaz for Ruth, the Lord provided family (and ultimately love and protection) for me in His way, and in His very specific time. Blue Eyes now picks our five-year-old daughter up from kindergarten, buckles her into her car seat, asks her how her day was, then takes her home and feeds her good things, helps her with her homework, and tucks her into bed at a reasonable hour.

I grew up with instability, but now, I get a front-row seat to stability. Our God is small-picture kind, and big-picture faithful.

Redemption is God's specialty. But not in the way we might think. It would be tidy for me to close this part of my story with an "everything happens for a reason" platitude, because—how perfect is it that I had to leave my safe life to meet the love of my life?

But the truer Truth is this: God's covenant promises are even better than that.

It's true that God specializes in redeeming stories and people. (He gave me an ending and a beginning all in the same week!) But there's even more to it than that. God isn't simply in the business of redeeming our stories—He's in the business of redeeming the whole story. While our stories are constantly changing, constantly ebbing and flowing with great news and crippling tragedy, He is unchanging. Permanent.

Celebrating the good moments is good, but let's learn to celebrate the broken ones, too. Sometimes, by God's sweet grace, the hard stuff is also the most worth-it stuff. Because of God's proven faithfulness to us, His people, we can put our hands squarely on each other's shoulders, look one another in the eye, and remind each other that God is at work. Without a doubt. Redemption is always coming.

WHAT'S IN YOUR CUP?

I want you to do something with me today.

I know we've just met, but I have an idea that we might all feel a little more comfortable if we end this chapter in a living room setting.

Let's say there are a dozen of us (Amanda is here, too! Everyone say, "Hi Amanda!") and we're all at my house—on sofas, in chairs, or on the floor leaning against the legs of a close friend. It's not a Bible study; it's just what we in the South like to call a "y'all come."

A lucky one of you is snuggled up next to our old Weimaraner, Scout, who has likely inched her way off of her "place" and nearly into the lap of the first guest who made the mistake of patting her head and telling her she's a good girl. You and Scout are friends for life, and I apologize for that. I can put her in the other room if you want.

Here we all are. I'm not feeling super polished today, but a glance around the room makes me feel like I'm not alone. We've all arrived in varying states of "together-ness" and something about that feels very honest. It's a safe place, and the fact that my hair is unwashed and I'm sans makeup today is my own particular flavor of hospitality.

We all have mugs in our hands because that's what we do. My mug cabinet has hit a point of excess (perhaps you have this problem, too?), and I happily let everyone take their pick. I have a bunch of She Reads Truth mugs in there (perks of the job), so a few of you pick those. I choose one with a photo of my son Oliver on it, and a lucky one of you gets the "grog" mug my husband inherited from his Grandma Posey's kitchen. It's cloudy white glass made into the shape of a troll-ish face. It makes no sense to me, but that's the mug our guests always reach for.

One thing I like about having friends over is getting to know how everyone likes their coffee. Me? I always add a bit of flavored creamer, plus a splash of half-and-half. If Blue Eyes were around, he'd offer to make lattes or Americanos with his espresso machine, but since there are a dozen women in his living room, there's a solid chance he's made himself scarce.

Tea or water, black coffee or mostly creamer—as we sit around the living room, we all have something in our cups.

But let's pretend for a minute that our carefully chosen mugs aren't actually filled with beverages. Instead, we each look down into the cups we're holding to see our present circumstances.

One of you just got a new job and we are geeked for you! (I grew up in Michigan, and when we were excited, we were "geeked.")

Another one of you just had a new baby—congrats! And, bless your heart, you must be exhausted.

That's what's in your mugs.

But I see one of you sitting in the chair by the fireplace, looking down into your mug, unable to lift your eyes. You miscarried last month and don't really know how to process it, let alone bring it up in a room full of women who are celebrating someone else's baby. Not wanting to be the downer, you just keep quiet and hope nobody notices.

I see another one of you over there on the sofa. You took your first job out of college this fall and you're unexpectedly very lonely. You thought a job that allowed you to "work remotely" sounded free and fun, but instead you spend your days alone and you feel more isolated than you've ever felt in your entire life, away from home and in a new city.

Then there's one of you by the window. Your husband just lost his job and you're facing serious financial strain. The thought of losing your home or moving to another town has you devastated and a little desperate. It breaks your heart to think of how uncertain your life has become.

One of you asks me what's in my cup and I almost wish you hadn't. My kids are in school and I'm working full-time. I've been achy lately, missing the simpler days of being at home with my babies, painting furniture and taking walks. I've got a heaping helping of transition in my cup, and if I'm honest, a hard obedience to God's calling on my life in this season. I'm ashamed to admit how often it keeps me up at night.

Finally, we've all named what's on our hearts. Even the ones of us who didn't want to go at first got brave and shared, and we are glad we did. Now we're all quietly looking into our cups, staring our present circumstances in the face, unaware of just how temporary they really are. They feel permanent to us. We may not be alone in our burdens, but we feel them pressing down on us just the same.

This is the moment I imagine Jesus meeting each of us as if we're the only one in the room. He reaches out to touch your face, lifts your chin until your eyes meet His, and you understand one thing for the first time or the hundredth; the truth in your cup is nothing compared to the truer Truth that is looking you in the face at that moment.

"Come to Me," He says (Matt. 11:28).

"My peace I give to you" (John 14:27).

"You will be My people, and I will be your God" (Jer. 30:22).

And for a moment, we forget about our circumstances—our loneliness, our transitions, our exciting news, and our devastating losses. For a moment, with our eyes fixed on the truest Truth, we see the big stuff of life for the temporary that it is. When we lock eyes with the One who is permanent, the only thing that overwhelms us is a peace that passes understanding.

Those things in our cups don't disappear. That's not why we feel peace. We'll all return today to our broken relationships and endless to-do lists, our personal crises and our big plans that we know in our hearts are shaky at best. All of these things are still real, still true. While the contents of our cups are different, Jesus Christ is the same—yesterday, today, and forever (Heb. 13:8). He will always be truer and more lasting than anything that will ever find its place in our cups.

It's getting late, so we set our mugs on the counter, hug good-bye, and walk out the door. But now, no matter what we're walking back into, we walk in the freedom of the Truth. In a world that's perpetually passing away, we've found something Permanent. Jesus doesn't stop lifting our gaze to Him.

1 CORINTHIANS 13:8–12 ESV

Love never ends. As for prophecies, they will pass away; as for tongues, they will cease; as for knowledge, it will pass away. For we know in part and we prophesy in part, but when the perfect comes, the partial will pass away. When I was a child, I spoke like a child, I thought like a child, I reasoned like a child. When I became a man, I gave up childish ways. For now we see in a mirror dimly, but then face to face. Now I know in part; then I shall know fully, even as I have been fully known.

THE STACK

God's Promises Are Permanent
When the World's Promises Pass Away

I have a thing in my life that feels permanent. I call it "The Stack."

I'm referring to the mound of miscellany that lives on the far corner of our kitchen counter. You're bound to see it if you come visit because our front door is merely a formality. The only reasonable way to enter our home is by the entrance at the carport, where the broken screen door slams so loudly you'll be sure you broke it. (Don't worry. It's been that way for months.)

That broken door leads you into the mudroom, which leads you into the kitchen, which is where you'll see The Stack, dead ahead and to the right. This is why I'll think twice before inviting you over—not because I don't want to let you in, but because I know it means that pile of life-stuff will be found out. It's like that dream in Junior High where you show up at the school assembly naked, but it's my lack of order that's exposed, all in one disorganized heap.

The Stack is ever-present and impossible to hide. It is the bits and pieces of life, the things that find their way in the door each day but don't yet have a place to go. There are party invitations and "Save the Date" cards, utility bills and bank statements, sheets upon sheets of completed schoolwork dragged out of the backpacks of two kindergarteners and their third-grade big sister. There are broken toys to repair, markers with missing tops, and a tiny lightbulb I can't find a replacement for to save my life.

This unsightly pile is a snapshot into my life, an endless collection of facts:

4+4=8.

Yes, we will attend the party next Saturday.

We owe $82.60 to the electric company.

This toy is broken (again).

Facts though they may be, the items in this collection are always changing. More paper floods in to replace any I manage to file or throw away. There are new bills to pay, more lists to check off, and more to-dos to get done. No matter how diligently I try to sort through it all—organizing, eliminating, reconciling—it's still there at the end of the day to taunt me and greet my guests as they walk in the door.

Facts are facts, and they are ever-changing in The Stack just like they're ever-changing in our lives.

Truth is different. Truth remains.

When those little life-facts fly in the door and onto The Stack, they each bring spoken or unspoken promises along with them. The math worksheets will teach my boys to add. Attending that party will help us stay connected to the people we love. Paying the power bill will keep the lights on. Supergluing that broken toy for the third time will please my daughter (and hopefully produce more patience in her mama).

These promises are flimsy on a good day. They're just the stuff of life—mostly mundane. But that doesn't stop me from arranging my life around them and hoping for the best. I make sure the kids do their homework. I try to be a good friend by RSVPing before the deadline. By the grace of God, the utility bills get paid. And I expect life to go a certain way in return. The promises that mound holds aren't certain by any means, but that doesn't stop me from treating them like guarantees.

Most days, my Bible sits on that same counter. I toss it there with my bag as I rush in the door from work. The Bible, too, is a collection of facts and promises. Here are just a few:

Jesus was there when the Earth was formed. "In the beginning was the Word" (John 1:1).

Jesus died a real, physical death on the cross. "He said, 'It is finished!' Then bowing His head, He gave up His spirit" (John 19:30).

Jesus' blood atones for our sins. "We have redemption in Him through His blood, the forgiveness of our trespasses, according to the riches of His grace . . ." (Eph. 1:7).

Jesus will be back. "Look, I am coming quickly!" (Rev. 22:7).

Seeing my messy pile of world-promises next to God's book of eternal covenant, it's clear the mistake I've made. I've come to expect the same thing from God's promises as I do the world's, treating them both like they're unshakable. Even worse, I'm prone to see the world-promises as sure footing while suspecting the Scripture-promises may shift.

The world's promises to me and God's promises to the world—they sit side by side on my kitchen counter, but they are far from equal.

OUR PROMISES VS. GOD'S PROMISES

We learned early into life with Baby No. 1 to be very careful when making promises to children. They can detect a shift in the wind faster than a reputable meteorologist, and they will not hesitate to call you on it.

Now, three kids in, we make only one promise to our children: "I love you always and forever, no matter what." I know there will be days when even that promise will be tough to keep, but any lesser promise is out of the question. I will not promise to take you to a particular restaurant, because restaurants sometimes close. In fact, I may not promise to take you to a restaurant at all. I will not promise that you can sleep over at your friend's house next weekend because her family's plans might change and so may ours. And I will not promise to play that game with you after dinner because you may throw spaghetti at your sister during said dinner. But I will love you, all the time. Period. The end.

God's promises to us, thankfully, are different than a parent's promises to her children, not just in substance but in essence. Because God is who He is—good, holy, faithful, just—His promises are, by nature, unbreakable. His promises are part of a covenant, an everlasting, overarching capital-P Promise to His people. The promises are true because the Promise is true.

When I need proof of the Promise—which is every single day—I turn to Scripture. I read Truth.

I read about the God who created mankind from dust and in love, sealing that love with a promise, and not withdrawing when they rebel against Him:

> "I will put hostility between you and the woman, and between your seed and her seed. He will strike your head, and you will strike his heel." (Gen. 3:15)

Spoken by God Himself to the lying serpent that tempted the man and woman to sin, this vow is our first glimpse of the covenant the

Creator established with His creation: "I will not leave you to your sin. I will rescue you."

I see the covenant continue with Noah as a holy God wiped the earth clean of rampant evil, but not before stretching out His hand to cover one imperfect, capable-of-evil family:

> "Understand that I am bringing a flood—floodwaters on the earth to destroy every creature under heaven with the breath of life in it. Everything on earth will die. But I will establish My covenant with you, and you will enter the ark with your sons, your wife, and your sons' wives." (Gen. 6:17–18)

I read, in awe, as God so poetically conveyed His covenant to Abraham, taking him outside to gaze at the stars and saying to him, "Your offspring will be that numerous" (Gen. 15:5).

And then to David, the shepherd boy God plucked from the pasture to rule over Israel, God confirmed His covenant once more:

> "The LORD declares to you: The LORD Himself will make a house for you. When your time comes and you rest with your fathers, I will raise up after you your descendant, who will come from your body, and I will establish his kingdom. He will build a house for My name, and I will establish the throne of his kingdom forever." (2 Sam. 7:11–13)

In the pages of Scripture, we see God's covenant passed down from generation to generation, perfectly kept along the way and made new in the life, death, and resurrection of Jesus.

At the Last Supper with His disciples, Jesus gave thanks and broke the bread, saying, "This is My body, which is given for you." Then after supper He took the cup and held it up, saying, "This cup is the new covenant established by My blood" (Luke 22:19–20).

The new covenant in Christ still holds, from that supper table in Jerusalem to us here today.

Being human through and through and nothing close to divine, my promises stand weak and wobbly next to the covenant of the almighty God. The closest thing I have to a covenant-caliber promise here on earth are my wedding vows, made on a breezy September afternoon on a hillside in Franklin, Tennessee.

I'd only known David, my groom, for a year and two months before that day, but we pledged all the days of the rest of our life to one another without a hint of uncertainty. This was a noteworthy occasion by any measure. It was especially so considering my love-hate relationship with commitment, as unpredictable as the late-summer weather in middle Tennessee. But the sun shone that day and 100 of the people we loved most sat in the shade of a small white tent. I walked the grass aisle on my father's arm while the hammered dulcimer played, and we promise-breakers made our lofty promise to each other, fully meaning every word.

The marriage covenant my husband and I made to each other is not guaranteed to hold, as much as we wish it were and truly believe it will. That glue currently keeping my daughter's favorite toy together isn't guaranteed to hold either. "There's no such thing as a guarantee," the world generally agrees, and we know from experience that it's true. But that's not the stuff wedding homilies are made of. That's not what we want to believe.

We know promises are good. We know they are meant to be kept. But schedules shift and toys break. Contracts fall through and, heartbreakingly, marriages sometimes do too.

You and I were made for an unbreakable promise. We can have a guarantee. But we won't find it shoved in a windowed envelope on our messy countertop, or even in a tuxedoed groom. The one true covenant comes from the one true God, and we'll find it in His Word.

ZOOM OUT

Details make me nervous.

I like to know what to expect, but only generally. Tell me everything is going to be okay and a summary about why, and I'm a happy camper. Give me a list of specific details and my eyes will start to glaze over as an act of self-preservation. This is likely why I'm the worst at making plans. Zooming in makes me nervous. Zooming out reminds me that the details are just that—details.

Despite my detail aversion, once in a blue moon my plans pan out. It happened last summer when I successfully planned our first family vacation ever, to none other than a dude ranch. Whatever it is you're picturing right now—chaps and cowboy hats, barn dances and cattle drives—let me assure you, it was all of that and more.

My daughter was seven at the time and proud as punch to have her "own" horse for the week. Sporting a broad-brimmed hat, a T-shirt that read "bon voyage" in glitter, and jeans tucked into her riding boots, she was ready to become an honest-to-goodness cowgirl and totally looked the part. Her little brothers watched in awe as she walked confidently to the "big kids" corral. That's where she met Sparky.

Sparky was a mellow horse with a silky brown coat and a white patch above his eyes. He was short enough for a petite second grader to climb on from the woodblock step, but tall enough to make her eyes grow wide once she was in the saddle. Wide eyes quickly gave way to worry, which turned into mild panic. Gentle horse and friendly wranglers aside, our girl was not okay with the high-horse situation.

David and I spent two days trying to convince our daughter to ride her horse, and every eager counselor at the ranch chimed in to do the same. Each morning she'd bravely mount Sparky, her small hands with a death grip on the reins, and we'd watch them nervously trot down the trail. But then when lunchtime rolled around, we would see them walking slowly back to the corral, Sparky's reins held by a patient wrangler who'd offered to lead our anxious girl safely home.

It took us a while to understand what was going on in that little head of hers. Our firstborn is a spunky one. She's bold, larger-than-life. And here she was amid the beautiful mountains of Colorado, handed an opportunity she'd dreamt of for years. But she just couldn't do it. Her fear was getting the best of her and, for the life of us, we couldn't figure out why.

The answer began to reveal itself on Day Two. She stayed back from the afternoon ride, in tears of fear and frustration. "What is it, sweetie?" I asked for the umpteenth time. "I saw you up on that horse—you can do this! Why are you afraid?"

My precious child spouted off every bad scenario that could possibly take place when a human rides a horse. She could fall off, of course, but that wasn't all. The horse could run away. She might not be able to stop the horse. The horse might not be strong enough to hold her. What if the horse has a hurt leg and she doesn't know it? The horse could trip on a root, or jump over a creek, or just fall right there on the trail for no reason at all. Her heart and mind would not release her from the possibilities.

My sweet girl was letting the beaucoup of things that could—possibly—go wrong dictate her direction. In zeroing in on what seemed like concrete, indisputable facts (such as, "falling off a horse hurts"), she'd missed other facts altogether (like, "most people here won't fall off a horse at all" and "going fast on a horse is fun!"). Most importantly, she let her worry over the facts distract her from the larger truth: she'd always wanted to learn to ride, and this was her chance to do it.

The phrase "like mother, like daughter" was made for situations just like this. I'm one who's inclined to identify all the what-ifs of a situation and let them determine my course. I've been known to leave the question of "What's actually true here?" out of the equation altogether, assuming my assessment of the facts is really all that matters. And, like my girl, I can't seem to magically erase my fear just because someone tells me I ought to.

This world is ever-changing. It's passing away, and I can sense it, I can see it. Calculating the risks and evaluating my next steps are my ways of holding tight to the reins. In fact, I can grow so consumed with the calculating and the evaluating and the holding tight that I let go of the reason it all matters to begin with. When I focus on "just the facts," I forget the truest Truth.

When I'm zoomed in on my fear, I can't see the faithfulness of God and the steadfastness of His covenant.

When I'm determined to figure out my piece of the puzzle, I fail to see how the picture has been steadily coming together since the beginning of time.

When I grip too tightly the things I think I control, I lose touch of the eternal Truth that it is God who holds all things together.

But when I zoom out to see the fullness of God's promises—to remember His covenant that He has upheld for generation after generation—the Truth comes into view. Only then do I see that those blurry parts of the picture do not change the glory of the whole. The uncertain places that I want so desperately to bring into focus do not change what is truly true.

Our girl did learn to ride her horse. But it wasn't just because we said she could; it was because she looked around and saw she could. She saw other girls and boys riding their horses, and she listened to us explain that the falling was unlikely but also worth it. She heard our words and believed they were true, but she also tried on the truth for herself.

On Day Three, she got back in the saddle and rode. She did the same on Day Four, her confidence growing a smidgen with every trip. That afternoon, we went to the top of the mountain together—my daughter, her dad, and me. She was still afraid but she was moving, every step a success story.

I watched as she began to steal glimpses of the world around the trail, looking up quickly and then back down to Sparky's mane. Like her mom, she was learning to believe in the truth she could not see—by taking one step and then another.

At the top of the mountain, we stopped and stood our horses in a row. And there, flanked on either side by the humans who love her most, our daughter relaxed her grip on the reins and looked full at the 180-degree view. The fear had not disappeared from her eyes, but it paled next to the sparks of joy and wonder.

BOTH/AND

When I think of that time on the ranch, I don't roll my eyes at my daughter's fears. They were not irrational thoughts to be conquered or impossibilities to be dismissed. Her fears were real. Mine and yours are too. Pretending they aren't would be unreasonable.

Our circumstances are also real. The anxiety I couldn't shake as I lay in bed last night was real. The pain your body feels from illness, or the tragedy your family has endured, or the financial hole you're digging out of—those are real too. The facts in our lives that we try to keep orderly and under control, that we use to measure our days, do not disappear or change just because we will them to.

Trusting in God's Truth does not mean ignoring everything else. We do not have to explain our fears away in order to earnestly believe God's promises to us. It is not an either/or situation. It is both/and.

We are afraid, AND God is trustworthy.

Awful things happen, AND God is wholly good.

We are sick, AND Jesus is the Great Physician.

The world is passing away, AND God's kingdom will stand.

Truth is not diminished when we stand it next to our doubts, questions, and fears.

On the last day of our visit to the ranch, David and I rode with a group up to a peak called Hounddog Rock. The ride was even more eventful than usual as we led our horses along the edge of a cliff-like embankment, the creek below moving swiftly with more rain in weeks than it normally sees in months. My horse, Phoebe, liked her place at the back of the pack, and after six days together I still couldn't coerce her to venture ahead of the others.

The second half of the trail took us up a steeper portion of the mountain, and we zigzagged our way through the rocks and the trees that had been burned down to their charcoal-black trunks. We'd heard bits and pieces about the devastating fire of several years ago, spotting evidence of the flames on each winding trail. But we'd seen nothing that compared to what we saw from Hounddog Rock.

We reached the top of the peak, and I tied Phoebe's lead to a nearby tree trunk. Climbing up on a rock to get a better view, I plopped down next to David, stretching my tired legs out in front of me. Then I looked up.

There, all around us, was the massive footprint of the fire. I'd never seen anything like it.

I took in the panoramic view, tracing the outline of the fire's domain like a map in my mind. Inside the invisible boundary the landscape was wiped clean of everything green. Only rocks remained—rocks and black tree stumps like the ones we'd ridden through all week. Literally nothing else.

The devastation, though vast, was to be expected. What left me speechless was the beauty.

The flames had devoured the vegetation, but the majesty of the mountains stood firm. The fire had destroyed thousands and thousands of acres of trees, and the rocks remained unchanged.

TRUTH REMAINS

Like the rock that withstands the raging fire, the Truth will remain. Everything around it will perish, but the Truth—and the One who gives it—will remain.

The prophet Isaiah stated it plain as day: "The grass withers, the flowers fade, but the word of our God remains forever" (Isa. 40:8). Jesus, standing on a mountain, said the same to His disciples: "Heaven and earth will pass away, but My words will never pass away" (Matt. 24:35). And listen to these no-nonsense words from Peter's second letter: "But the Day of the Lord will come like a thief; on that day the heavens will pass away with a loud noise, the elements will burn and be dissolved, and the earth and the works on it will be disclosed" (2 Pet. 3:10).

The facts of our lives will melt away with the heat; they were never meant to last. But when the trappings of this temporary life burn away, what will be revealed? Is my life hidden in the immovable, imperishable rock of God and His Word, or am I climbing hills made of lesser things and hoping for the best?

One day, eternity will set fire to The Stack that plagues my kitchen counter. (Or maybe that could happen today? I'm not much for pyrotechnics, but this, I could get behind.) All those bills, that clutter, those to-dos will one day burn up and dissolve into nothing. So what does that mean for me and you today? Do we throw up our hands and mutter, "Well, it's all gonna pass away eventually anyway"? Or do we dig in deeper to that which lasts?

Let's ignore the pat answers and humor the question for a while. It's one I've asked myself more times than I care to admit.

If I torched that pile of papers on my countertop, there would be some consequences, though none of them dire. I would forget my eye appointment and the kids would miss that bowling party. Unpaid bills would leave our house dark and cold for the winter, but we could light some candles

34

and bundle up to get by. There'd be some drama from the kids over the handful of lost art pieces, but that would be followed by a round of high fives when they realized the homework assignments had disappeared. The cause would have its various effects, but nothing eternal would change.

If the stuff of life will burn away, why can't I ignore the cares of today and simply hold out for the eternal tomorrow?

I could, were it not for Jesus.

Jesus knew exactly how temporary the things of this world are. He was "with God in the beginning," after all, and "all things were created through Him" (John 1:2–3). Even so, "He emptied Himself . . . taking on the likeness of men," the Creator becoming like one of His created for the sake of reconciling them eternally to Himself (Phil. 2:7). He was Emmanuel, God truly with us.

The Son of God came to earth to die in our stead. Who would have blamed Him for biding His time until the end?

But that's not who Jesus was. Ignoring the world around Him would not have brought glory to His Father. And ignoring the people around Him was not in His nature—a nature defined by love and holiness, justice and grace.

Instead of keeping His distance, the Son of God did the opposite: He fully entered in.

Jesus attended weddings and cooked breakfast. He started conversations with strangers and fed hungry crowds. He embraced lepers and healed the hurting. He took notice of widows and sat orphans on His knee. He wept with His friends and He loved His mama.

Jesus knew precisely what would and wouldn't last, and He chose to be all here. He chose to be fully present, out of obedience to His Father and love for His people. As followers of Christ, we are called to do the same.

The knowledge that this world is temporary, and the affirmation that only God and His Word are eternal, is not a license to give up on life as we know it. It is not our permission slip to care only about the everlasting life while harboring indifference toward this passing one. No, this knowledge is both an invitation and a mandate to dig in deeper—to live our earthly lives in earnest, in light of eternity.

God's Truth gives our temporary lives eternal significance. It speaks forgiveness over our sin, hope over our despair, worth over our shame, and life over our death. In its light, everything matters. And at the same time, nothing else matters.

In light of God's Truth, we can zoom in on the details of this life without being ruled by uncertainty and fear. And in light of God's Truth, we can zoom out to see the whole, God-sized picture, knowing He and His Word will outlast anything we can see or control.

In the surety of God's love, we can let up on the reins of our everyday and enjoy the panoramic view of His covenant faithfulness, stretching as far as the eye can see. And we also have the freedom to lean in close to engage a friend's specific joy, panic, or pain, knowing that our infinite God cares for even the finite details of His children's lives.

With Jesus, it's both/and.

But one day we won't need both/and.

When the temporary has passed away, when The Stack and every other finite thing has finally returned to dust, we'll be left standing face-to-face with the Permanent One. There will be no more guesswork then.

We won't wonder if it was worth it to sacrifice our comforts for the sake of those souls who walked around us, clothed in temporary bodies. We'll know. We won't worry that we should have climbed those mountains made of self and stuff. They'll be gone. We won't question the trustworthiness of our covenant-making Creator and His every word. We'll see it all clearly.

When all is stripped away from our lives, one foundation will be revealed. May it be Him.

SHE READS TRUTH

2 CORINTHIANS 1:19–22 ESV

For the Son of God, Jesus Christ, whom we proclaimed among you, Silvanus and Timothy and I, was not Yes and No, but in him it is always Yes. For all the promises of God find their Yes in him. That is why it is through him that we utter our Amen to God for his glory. And it is God who establishes us with you in Christ, and has anointed us, and who has also put his seal on us and given us his Spirit in our hearts as a guarantee.

2 PETER 3:8–13

Dear friends, don't let this one thing escape you: With the Lord one day is like a thousand years, and a thousand years like one day. The Lord does not delay His promise, as some understand delay, but is patient with you, not wanting any to perish but all to come to repentance.

But the Day of the Lord will come like a thief; on that day the heavens will pass away with a loud noise, the elements will burn and be dissolved, and the earth and the works on it will be disclosed. Since all these things are to be destroyed in this way, it is clear what sort of people you should be in holy conduct and godliness as you wait for and earnestly desire the coming of the day of God. The heavens will be on fire and be dissolved because of it, and the elements will melt with the heat. But based on His promise, we wait for the new heavens and a new earth, where righteousness will dwell.

REMEMBER WHOSE YOU ARE

God's Covenant Is Permanent
When Our Good Intentions Pass Away

I was fifteen the summer I stuck my True Love Waits commitment card in the ground of the Washington Mall with about ten thousand others. A sea of white index card-sized promises, glued to sticks and planted in the grass by teenagers from around the country, pledged that we would live out our devotion to Christ by guarding our hearts and bodies for marriage.

We were giving God a guarantee.

Four years earlier, I'd had my first kiss. It happened when I was eleven, beside the footbridge a few blocks from my house. The blonde-haired boy and I stood partially hidden in the vines at our appointed first-kiss location, while my friend watched and waited at a safe distance. There we stood, the boy and me, on the bank of the canal that ran through our small

Southern hometown, and together we experienced an awkward, staged kiss that my middle school vocabulary could only describe as "mushy."

He was a nice boy and I was a nice girl, and our curiosities seemed innocent enough. But that day at the footbridge awoke a need in me that no promise I made would be able to shake, not until the day my husband made vows to me more than a dozen years later. The need to be accepted and approved by handsome, decent boys would be my Achilles' heel, my sin of choice, the thing I clung to when my heart longed to feel loved, kept, safe.

I've made many other promises to God over my thirty-seven years, though few with the pomp of that pledge card in Washington, DC. My teens and early twenties boasted a collection of attempted guarantees among the standard tumult of a girl's teenage years. But the promise I stuck in that perfectly manicured, impossibly green grass is the one I think of most. It's the one that best embodies my struggle to be who I thought God needed me to be—unconflicted, tidy, resolved, capable of making God a promise and keeping it—while being who I actually was: a well-intentioned mess.

I think back on that sea of faces, the boys and girls who planted their paper promises next to mine, and I wonder how many of them were like me. I wonder if they, too, hung their spiritual hat on what they could do for God instead of what God had already done for them. I wonder if any of them are haunted years later by that white card stuck in the ground, a promise to their Creator that they didn't keep.

True love, as it turned out, did wait for me. But I didn't wait on true love.

As soon as the promise was made, the promise-breaking began. We'd driven from Alabama to DC in a Greyhound bus, which felt a little like heaven to a group of small-town church kids. Fourteen hours each way trapped in a rolling hangout room with some of my closest friends. And what did I do? Flirted with a boy. A boy I didn't even like that much. Oh, he was nice. And tan and tall. But I was much more interested in me than him. I was more interested in being seen by him than getting to know him, more intent on getting him to like me than thinking about whether or not I liked him. It was horribly selfish, but subtle enough that I never once thought of it as such.

The game continued in the weeks after we got home. I'd pursue the boy just to see if I could get him to pursue me back. I'd give away parts of my heart for no reason at all, too distracted by the prize of acceptance to realize an emotional depletion was taking place. If that pledge card was my promise, I was tearing at the corners bit by bit, all the while wondering why I never felt whole.

Even now, so many years removed, it is hard for me to explain the constant defeat I felt when it came to this area of my life. Repeated restarts, vowing to do better this time around. Feeling the insatiable need to be seen and known, then feeling shame for those very same things.

The cycle repeated, as if on a timer, sending me back to the drawing board again and again, each time feeling more fractured than the last. What a disappointment to God I must be—this was the thought on which I always landed.

I couldn't be worth much to God, I reasoned, being so hell-bent on failure. So I vacillated between searching for approval from boys and working overtime in the other direction, trying one more time to be worth something to God. What guarantees could I offer God so He could keep loving me? And what guarantees could I secure from the world around me to fill in the remaining gaps?

The search lasted a solid decade, the pendulum of my efforts swinging wildly in both directions. The Good Girl did all the good things she could think of to guarantee her goodness and the Secret Rebel did what was required of her to feel loved.

The Good Girl got good grades, had good friends, and was a good-standing member of all the good clubs. She turned in her homework on time, sang alto in the church youth choir, and worked part-time jobs to earn extra money. She rode around the streets of her small hometown on the weekends with her friends, singing loud to the music with the windows rolled down. But she stopped short of frequenting the abandoned parking lot near the dock, where the cool kids and the bad kids went to drink.

The Secret Rebel was exactly that, bending the rules and breaking her own heart in ways only some would know—ways I'm still embarrassed to admit. It hurts to think of her now, the girl I was, with so many years of experience and understanding now between us.

It's hard to watch her stay in the relationship with the respectable boy who did disrespectful things. It's hard to see her buckle under false obligations to the boy after that, spending herself piece by piece to pay the bill he insisted she owed. It's hard to see her tossed in the same cycle, year after year, boy after boy, always hoping that love offered would yield a guarantee of love in return.

It's hard to see that teenage girl hiding in a shack that shame built, too afraid of herself to come into the light.

She didn't know God's promises to her were not the same as the promises she made to Him. She didn't understand that His faithfulness was not dependent on hers. While she searched long and hard for guarantees, even fashioning some of her own, God was upholding the ultimate and only true guarantee. He was always and actively keeping His covenant of love to His children—to her.

She was Israel, giving her heart to idols. And He was faithful, pursuing her without pause. He kept her close. He still does.

> Therefore, this is what I will do:
> I will block her way with thorns;
> I will enclose her with a wall,
> so that she cannot find her paths.

She will pursue her lovers but not catch them;
she will seek them but not find them. (Hos. 2:6–7)

I can't go back and free that good-girl rebel from the shackles of her sin and striving. Present-day Amanda can't grab the teenage Amanda by the shoulders and look her in the eyes and tell her to stop searching the world for its guarantees—promises bound to be broken.

I can't persuade her to stop giving God guarantees, and to rest instead in the unbreakable promise He's already given. But I can hold tight to the Truth today, and I can hold tight again tomorrow. I can cease the search and rest my weary bones right here—in the right-now hope of the already-fulfilled promises of God.

BELONGING TO SOMEONE

If anyone other than Future Me could have convinced my teenage self to stop running after false guarantees, it was my mom.

Having come to faith as an adult, my mom has spent the decades since then bowing in earnest before the Lord. Early mornings, while it was still dark, you could find her in her chair, praying and meeting with God in His Word. She kept her denim-covered Good News Bible, published around the same year I was born, in a canvas case that zipped all the way closed, holding in the pages that had grown loose from years of turning.

Mom's mornings then looked like her mornings now—sitting in a chair in the quiet, Bible open and head bowed, layers of pencil markings in the margins where she'd connected people and prayers to passages and promises. A few years ago when I was helping her move, I came across a box of her prayer journals—notebooks I'd seen all my life, sitting next to that chair, now all gathered together in one large box. I spread them out on the floor so I could see the vastness of them, a legacy of promises believed.

It was those words she spoke to God, not the words she spoke to me, that challenged me the most. It was the way she lived out her belief—faithful, simple, steady—that helped me see that Truth was real. Her living, breathing faith was the primary instrument of God's love in my life.

It was also the light that most threatened to expose my darkness.

There are memories my mind has quieted for the sake of my heart, and try as I may, I can't unmute them. But there are others that refuse to be hidden—and this is one of those:

It was night and I was driving home from a place I should not have been, a place I didn't dare admit existed. It was someone's home, but I would never feel at home there. I would always feel like the imposter, unsafe, like a soldier venturing into enemy territory just to see what would happen.

But going there promised being seen and known, and so I willingly let down my guard.

Driving back home in my mom's van, the back roads were especially dark, with no street lamps to light my way. I was reeling from the mistakes I'd made—was actively making—and my body shifted into autopilot, van pointed toward home.

A flood of bright light through my driver's side window jolted me awake from my thoughts, and the blaring horn of a train followed long and loud. I snapped my right foot down to the floor without thinking, flying that white van over the railroad tracks just before the train barreled through. In my memory, the call was terrifyingly close. In reality, it was a tangible illustration of the choices I was making. I was looking for a safe place, but I was running willingly, repeatedly—and only somewhat naively—into danger to find it. I couldn't bring myself to pull the van over on that dark, unfamiliar road to regain my composure that night.

Heart racing, eyes glued to the blurry yellow lines in front of me, I wept openly in the driver's seat of my sweet mom's van all the way home.

Somewhere between that pledge card and those train tracks, my mom left me a note I'll never forget.

Notes on our kitchen counter were common. Mom was a teacher at my high school, and she would often work late for the sake of her students. Helping is just her way—she can't help but help. On nights when she was staying late for a club meeting or a tutoring session, she would leave us instructions for dinner prep: *Pinto beans on the stove are ready to warm. Mix the cornmeal with buttermilk for the cornbread. Don't forget to grease and preheat the skillet. XO*

Or, *Leftover roast in the fridge. See you soon, sugar babe. -Mae*

She still calls me Sugar Babe, and I'm happy to let her.

Notes were common at our house. But this next note was different. It was a note I'd never forget.

The particulars are fuzzy now, but I remember a few things clearly: I was going somewhere I knew I ought not be going. And I knew that my mom knew I ought not be going, even though I hadn't been forthright about the details. I'd told her a half-truth and she was onto me, but she did not accuse. She simply called my bluff, loving me hard but literally and figuratively letting me go where I was determined to go.

That evening I ran down the stairs to find the house empty on my way out—Dad was still at work and Mom had run an errand—and I found her note in the usual place on the kitchen counter. But this time, instead of a lighthearted letter signed with hearts or x's and o's, there were only four words in my mother's handwriting:

Remember whose you are.

I didn't need her there to explain what it meant. I knew. There were only four words on that paper, but I heard four more—unwritten but communicated clearly just the same.

"You belong to God. Remember Whose you are."

I heard my mother's words deep in the darkest, most self-neglected parts of my heart—I really did. It was the refrain I'd heard from her my whole life, and it was and still is true: "You are loved. You belong to Someone." But the lies echoed too, and I regularly soaked them in. Rather than trying to crowd the Truth out altogether, the Liar told my heart and head a deceitful story of "yes, but . . ."

The lie was a story I believed not only in thought but in action: "You are loved, but you must also seek out love wherever you can find it. You belong to Someone, but you cannot let yourself be alone. You may be God's, but you sure don't deserve to be."

Remembering that I belonged to God was the call I heard not just from the mother who loved me, but from a church who loved me too. It was the call I heard when I read my Bible and when I journaled my deepest prayers. It was the call I heard often enough to keep me tethered to the Truth by the thinnest of threads, by the grace I now see so clearly in retrospect. But the earnest belief that I had to earn my right to be God's left me feeling stuck. I could see with my eyes that large pieces of my life didn't line up with what I knew to be true, but I had no clue how to fix it.

If I was His, why did I try so hard only to fail so often? If I was His, why did I feel the need to belong to so many others? If I was His, why couldn't I walk out of this cycle I'd walked into?

If I was His, why did "Remember whose you are" sound more like a threat than a comfort?

THE ONE WHO STAYED

When my husband David and I were dating, he gave me a stack of five CDs. "I can't bear knowing that you don't own these albums. Here, I got these for you." He said it with kindness, a note of giddiness in his voice and not a trace of judgment. He loved that music so much, and he was beginning to love me too. He needed us to know each other, the music and me.

I was listening to one of those albums in my car the day it first occurred to me: I'm going to marry this guy. There I sat, parked in the gravel lot in front of my apartment, while Marc Cohn sang the ballad "True Companion" through the speakers of my Mazda 626. I started sobbing somewhere around the third verse, the one about how he's determined, in the most endearing way, that this woman he's singing to will one day be his bride.

I sobbed because I knew it: David was choosing me to be his girl in white. Only, I didn't feel worthy of being chosen. I still don't, if I'm honest. I know me, and I know that I'm not the girl I promised to be the day I signed that pledge card in the summer of '94. I was a wreck. I was a runaway train who'd managed to find the brakes because this amazing Air Force vet with combed-back hair and vintage button-down shirts had me completely smitten. But what if the brakes gave way again? What if I started careening back down that familiar road, picking up speed and sideswiping everything good we'd been given in our three short months together?

I was still that wreck of a girl. What if I wrecked this too?

David and I were nothing but honest with each other from our very first date. He'd invited me to go with him to a benefit dinner, and I happily accepted the invitation, not even bothering to hide the smile that was plastered on my face most of the night. I remember how taken aback I was with the way he talked, so fast and intense. I remember how he was so focused on our conversation that he missed our exit and circled halfway around downtown Nashville before he realized it.

He was not the person I thought he was. I'd pegged him as aloof and a little arrogant, and it still makes me grin to think of how completely wrong I was. He was everything I didn't know to ask for in a boyfriend.

I was caught off guard and, frankly, pretty terrified at how my heart was responding to this man who dared to act like one.

I never had to wonder how David felt about me—not because he told me, but because he showed me. His interest in me came with a rare kind of resolve that made me feel both nervous and safe, in exactly the right ways. Even before that first chatty ride around the city in his well-loved, worn-in Bronco, I sensed in David an integrity that challenged me even as it drew me in. I was indeed smitten, but I wasn't sure what to do with him and his surety. Since we were always honest with each other, I told him so.

This was the point at which I would normally pull, if not run, away from the relationship. I knew the wrecking I was capable of and the heart-ache that would inevitably follow. In all my years of seeking promises of love and acceptance only to have them break apart, I'd learned not to trust anyone too much—most of all myself.

I tried to freak out, to give in to my fear of getting too close and being too vulnerable. I tried to convince David that this wouldn't work, not with me—the broken girl who breaks things. And I expected him to comply. I expected him to give me space, to back far enough away to save face in case I ran away. But true to form, he did what I least expected: he stayed. He waited patiently but he kept close. He didn't try to talk me out of my fear or reason away my uncertainty, and he didn't pretend he was unsure in turn. He simply stayed and kept loving me, brokenness and all.

David's feelings for me were truly independent of my feelings for him. He didn't stay because he was afraid of losing me. He stayed because he loved me, all of me. My fear and doubt couldn't change that. And because he stuck by his promise, I was eventually able to trust him and myself enough to make my own.

I love my husband. As evidenced by my gushing, I think he is objectively terrific. In many ways, I see how God used David's boldness and resolve to save me from what, based on my history, could have been.

But David's commitment to me is still only a faint image of the ultimate promise: God's covenant to us as His people.

The book of Hosea offers a heartbreaking glimpse into the reality of Israel's rebellion against God, like an adulterous wife who refuses the steadfast affection of her one true love. It also portrays the love and patience of the God who pursues His people, though they've done nothing but push Him away.

> Therefore, I am going to persuade her, lead her to the wilderness, and speak tenderly to her. There I will give her vineyards back to her and make the Valley of Achor into a gateway of hope. There she will respond as she did in the days of her youth, as in the day she came out of the land of Egypt. (Hosea 2:14–15)

The covenant love of our heavenly Father toward His people is so great, our former, false loves become a forgotten memory. Our idols evaporate when exposed to the affection of our truest Love, like a morning mist that hovers over the water only to be dissolved in the light of noonday sun.

> For I will remove the names of the Baals from her mouth; they will no longer be remembered by their names. (Hosea 2:17)

We can stop chasing lesser affections, stop trying to make ourselves worthy of love. Jesus has declared us worthy. The matter has been settled.

"He made the One who did not know sin to be sin for us, so that we might become the righteousness of God in Him" (2 Cor. 5:21).

The one true and holy God does not love us because we love Him. He loves us first (1 John 4:19).

He doesn't demand perfection from us and then stand, arms crossed and toe tapping, to see how we'll mess it up this time. He is patient with us, desiring for all to come to the knowledge of Him (2 Pet. 3:9; Isa. 30:18).

He made His covenant with us at the very beginning, choosing His Son to be our Savior before the foundation of the earth (1 Pet. 1:20).

In other words, God's covenant to us is not dependent on us. Not even a little bit. His guarantee is permanent, even when nothing we can muster in response is.

His love for me was sealed before He created me (Eph. 1:4–6). His love for you was set in eternal motion before you were knit together in your mother's womb (Ps. 139:13). It has been in place and upheld throughout every moment of every day of every year of our lives, generation after generation. How could it possibly depend on us?

God's covenant was true every time I looked elsewhere for love and acceptance. His covenant has been true every time you've acted out of fear and doubt. It is still true, no matter the circumstances we face or the hurt we hold in our hearts. Even when the temporary feels painfully permanent, His covenant is true.

Remember whose you are.

PERMISSION GRANTED

I've been a believer in Jesus since I was five years old.

Back before the pledge card, before the footbridge, before any real searching for guarantees from myself or anyone else, something simple and wonderful happened: God called my name and I answered. Like flabbergasted Moses staring at the burning bush, I did not know exactly what was happening or exactly what it meant, but I was certain in my willing, young heart that it was God who was doing the calling.

We were standing toward the front of our United Methodist chapel, singing from a hymnbook in the pews, my mom and my brother and me. I don't remember what preceded the moment, but I remember feeling sure that Jesus was real. And I remember feeling sure that I wanted to serve

Him. So I closed my eyes and held out my hands, palms up, like I was holding a serving tray. It was exhilarating.

This was my version of "Here I am" (Exod. 3:4). This was childlike faith in its uncomplicated beauty.

As I grew, my faith grew too. We attended church regularly, and I was as involved as I could be. I went to Sunday school and Bible studies and, yes, summer youth trips. I read the Bible outside of church too. I began to journal my prayers. But even as I became more sure of who God was, I became less sure of who I was in relation to Him. The little girl who stood unabashedly before God, eager hands ready to serve, became a teenager who hid like Mother Eve beneath fig leaves of shame.

It was no longer Moses' "Here I am" that I echoed in my heart; it was also his disbelief, "Who am I that I should go?" Or, as was more accurate to my line of thinking at the time: Who am I that I am worth loving?

My mom went with my youth group to a conference once that featured a concert by Todd Proctor. (I think Todd Proctor is a pastor now, but in the early '90s, he was a singer who played Christian youth events—a "worship artist" before we called them that.) My sweet mom was super into it. She loved that I loved Jesus and music and spending so much time with my church friends. She loved me, and she wanted me to feel loved, even more by God than by her. I told you. She's amazing like that.

At the Todd Proctor concert, my mom bought me a Witness Wear T-shirt—Christian T-shirts that were all the rage when I was "coming up," as the generation above me would say. I had multiple Witness Wear T-shirts in my wardrobe, and they said things like this: "Go against the flow" (an ichthus "fish" swimming in the opposite direction of an ocean full of other fish), the full verse of Philippians 4:13, and, my favorite, "Lord's Gym: His pain, your gain." (I know.)

My new T-shirt, acquired at the Todd Proctor show, said this: I am fully accepted, deeply loved, and completely forgiven in Christ Jesus.

And I was. But I didn't believe it.

The fullness of the gospel had saved me, but I only seemed to remember half of it.

I knew I needed to be forgiven, but I couldn't believe I was.

I knew God's love was deep, but I thought my sin was deeper.

I knew Christ accepted me, but I didn't imagine He'd accepted all of me.

I was a work in process, and I assumed the work was mine to complete. I was a well-intentioned mess, remember? I thought the mess was mine to clean up.

But guess what? That wasn't Truth. God never said I have to clean myself up before I come to Him, to get it right before I trust in Him. He never said I could not or would not be a work in process. Search for these commands in the Bible, and you will come up short.

In fact, God says the opposite.

The Bible is full of in-process people, those whom Christ pursued and loved exactly as they were, well-intentioned messes like me. Like you. If we need permission to be in process, we can look to Scripture.

I am the woman at the well, taken aback that this man would dare to be seen with me.

I am Zaccheus, standing at a distance and hoping to catch a glimpse of the Messiah.

I am Peter, promising I would never deny Him and then turning around to do exactly that.

I am Peter, weeping when I meet Jesus' eyes and realize that I have failed and failed big, again.

I am Martha, running around trying to guarantee my worth and everyone else's happiness.

I am Mary, collapsing at His feet because I am so desperate for His presence.

I am the adulterous woman, standing guilty for all the world to see.

I am the bleeding woman, utterly incapable of healing what ails me.

I am a mess, in process, just like all of them. Looking through its pages, I see pieces of me all through God's Book.

In God's Word I'm reminded that I don't secure my standing before Him by any guarantees I make, or even those I manage to keep. I am secure because He holds me in the safety of His covenant, the same covenant He has kept for generations past and will keep for generations to come.

The promises I make to God don't impress Him. They don't score bonus points in some heavenly account. Ultimately only one promise is necessary, only one guarantee is required: the promise He's made to me. And that promise has already been kept, sealed, for eternity. I can rest in it. I can stop making my own.

This is why I read Truth. The almost-truths bring striving, but the whole Truth brings life.

Before I graduated high school and headed to college, I had the words from my mom's note engraved on the inside of a silver ring: Remember whose you are. That ring had started out as my purity ring, the one I bought soon after making the promise to wait for true love. But a couple years later when I had Mom's words written inside, it became a symbol of so much more. It still stood for a promise, but it was God's promise to me.

True love was already mine. And I was always His.

SHE READS TRUTH

HOSEA 2:14-23

ISRAEL'S ADULTERY FORGIVEN

Therefore, I am going to persuade her,
lead her to the wilderness,
and speak tenderly to her.
There I will give her vineyards back to her
and make the Valley of Achor
into a gateway of hope.
There she will respond as she did
in the days of her youth,
as in the day she came out of the land of Egypt.
In that day—
    this is the LORD's declaration—
you will call Me, "My husband,"
and no longer call Me, "My Baal."
For I will remove the names of the Baals
from her mouth;
they will no longer be remembered by their names.
On that day I will make a covenant for them
with the wild animals, the birds of the sky,
and the creatures that crawl on the ground.
I will shatter bow, sword,
and weapons of war in the land
and will enable the people to rest securely.
I will take you to be My wife forever.
I will take you to be My wife in righteousness,
justice, love, and compassion.
I will take you to be My wife in faithfulness,

and you will know Yahweh.
On that day I will respond—
    this is the LORD's declaration.
I will respond to the sky,
and it will respond to the earth.
The earth will respond to the grain,
the new wine, and the oil,
and they will respond to Jezreel.
I will sow her in the land for Myself,
and I will have compassion
on No Compassion;
I will say to Not My People:
You are My people,
and he will say, "You are My God."

A BLUE-RIBBON GIRL

God's Love Is Permanent
When Our Good Behavior Passes Away

Even if the charge to "remember whose you are" is not a struggle for you, there is always the opposite danger of believing a life of obedience alone will keep you in good standing. But even an award-winning performance of coloring inside the lines cannot achieve what only Christ can award.

My baby-of-the-family response to my parents' divorce was a resolve to be good—maybe even great. I may not have been able to control what happened to my parents when I was little, but I was prepared to do my part to keep the rest of my life in order at any cost. I needed my world—a world that had shifted so much—to love me, and the best way I knew to get that love was to be the best student, citizen, and daughter I could be.

I'll never forget preparing for the 4th grade Speech Meet. I'd rehearsed my selection a hundred times: "Too Many Daves," by Dr. Seuss. I nailed not only the memorization of this masterpiece sonnet, but also the carefully thought-out inflections and facial expressions I was certain would seal the judges' affections. I was the kind of speaker they could be proud to have at the meet.

After weeks of practicing, the day of the Speech Meet finally arrived, and I delivered my monologue flawlessly. I may not have been the best speaker there (some kids had costumes!), but I won that blue ribbon. Even though dozens of other kids got blue ribbons too, it was the highest award possible, so I was pleased.

Just when I thought my "Too Many Daves" speech-giving career had peaked with the blue ribbon in our fancy private Christian school gymnasium, a letter arrived in the mail from my dad's yellow legal pad.

I'd received more than a hundred yellow letters in the year since my dad had gone to prison, several per week, in fact. Sometimes they were exciting to read—I loved mail! Other times, my tears would soak the pages knowing I had disappointed him even from a distance. I didn't write to him often enough and a lot of times I felt guilty as I folded his letters and filed them in a shoebox under my bed. Along with these yellow letters came the promises of new lawyers, court appeals, and innocence.

So many promises. So few of them kept.

One particular yellow letter closed with an invitation for my sister and me. Family visitation day was coming, and my stepmom and new baby half sister planned to drive eight hours with us to the Upper Peninsula of Michigan to visit our dad in prison. We would feel almost like a real family between the hours of 8 and 10 one Thursday morning next month.

A prison visit sounds awful now, but it was exciting to me then. I was ten and optimistic about appeals and whole families and all-we-could-eat gas station snacks. It was a chance for my dad to see how big I'd gotten. How smart I was. For him to be proud of me.

The day finally came. We were escorted through a series of security checkpoints as we entered the prison that Thursday morning. I remember carefully choosing just the right hat for my baby half sister to wear, but the guards took it away because it seemed like the kind of thing folks would use to sneak bad things through security. I laughed out loud to my stepmom—why would someone put a gun in the baby's hat?! My future as a criminal mastermind was dim.

We were seated at a table in a cinder block room, among other inmates and their guests at their own tables, guards keeping watch with loaded weapons. Even when my dad finally appeared and joined us at our table, it wasn't nearly the whole-family experience I'd envisioned when I read his letter.

First of all, there were so many serious guards. The room smelled terrible. The lighting was poor. And nobody even noticed the fashion pants I'd handpicked for what I thought would be a day of family fun. (They came with matching suspenders!) I could have gotten over all of these factors, but I soon realized I wasn't the only person my dad wanted to see during his limited visiting hours. He had a new wife and a new baby, so my sister and I waited our turns. We were disappointed to find that he wasn't actually all that interested in us.

I did finally get a chance to pipe into the conversation. And when you're ten, seeing your dad for the first time in a year under the surveillance of armed guards, you do what anyone in my situation would do—I started immediately in on my blue-ribbon speech:

> *Did I ever tell you that Mrs. McCave*
> *Had twenty-three sons and she named them all Dave?*
> *Well, she did. And that wasn't a smart thing to do.*
> *You see . . .*

And on I went, breathlessly performing my fancy-pants, fourth-grade heart out. Just as soon as I finished . . .

And one of them Zanzibar Buck-Buck McFate . . .
But she didn't do it. And now it's too late.

. . . My dad asked if I'd do it again—this time for some of the guards.
He wanted to show everyone how great I was!

There I stood, moments later, on a stage worlds away from my fourth-grade classroom, with an audience bearing very little resemblance to those polished parents with their reading glasses and coffee tumblers behind the judges' table at the Speech Meet. As I delivered this private performance in the family visitation room—inflections and faces and all—I didn't see guards or guns or the barbed wire just outside the windows. I tried not to think about how much I'd rather be spending our remaining time getting reacquainted with my dad, and simply accepted the opportunity to make him proud—to make him love me. I was all in.

To this day, it was probably the best performance of "Too Many Daves" any fourth grader has ever delivered to the inmates and guards at the Marquette Branch Prison. My dad's already-big smile was enormous. But as I watched his eyes, shifting from guard to guard, something clicked for the very first time—something that had been true for a long time. He wasn't proud of me—he was proud of him. He wasn't showing anyone how great I was—he was showing everyone how great he was. Worst of all, he wasn't interested in knowing me at all. Even at the tender age of ten, I began to understand what a lifetime would prove. He might never be interested in just me.

This was the story and the song of growing up the daughter of an imprisoned, manic-depressive father. Sometimes the yellow letters came every day; other times, weeks would pass without anything. Every word was always written in all caps. There was a lot about him, but very little about me.

Somehow, the season of the yellow letters and "Too Many Daves" pushed me to try even harder. First, to show him that he could be proud when he was ready to notice me, but eventually, to show my dad what he was missing. A blue-ribbon daughter he'd completely failed to see.

THE PRETTY ONE

Four years later, I had all of the charisma and impressionability of an eighth-grade early teenager. Dad was home from prison and a new baby half brother had been added to his family. Still believing we were the preferred "original children," my sister and I would grace the home of our dad's new family every other Sunday afternoon, dipping in and out of a life that was never quite ours.

One Sunday night we got special permission from Mom to stay past the court-mandated visiting time. A new pastor had come to serve the church we grew up in, and this would be his first evening in the pulpit.

When the service ended that night, we hung around the back of the sanctuary, waiting our turn to introduce ourselves to the new pastor and his family. Finally at the front of the line, my dad stood between my sister and me, then sort of pushed us in front of the pastor as if we were two guests at the royal ball, saying, "Pastor, I'd like you to meet my daughters. Raechel here is the pretty one, and Becky is the smart one."

I don't remember any words after that. I'm sure I said hello and pulled off whatever came next just fine. I was a pro when it came to poise, knowing all the right things to do, even in an awkward social situation. But I couldn't un-hear my dad's words.

Sitting in the passenger seat that night as my sister drove us home to our mom's house, I wondered for the first time why I never realized before that I was the "stupid one." Was I just pretty to him? After all this time?

A MODEL CITIZEN

Despite the underlying chaos of my private life, my public life was on point.

Very few of my friends even knew the messy parts of my family life, and I much preferred it that way. I managed to survive junior high with very few of the typical battle wounds so many of my friends incurred. One friend had a baby and a few others got into trouble with drugs, but I stayed in my lane and dug in to percussion, sentence diagramming, and my teal NIV Student Bible as our teachers warned us about being "Left Behind" and the dangers of "Sex, Drugs, and Rock and Roll."

I learned a lot of untruths about the Bible during these years. Mostly that my salvation was as fickle as my fourteen-year-old heart, and that my name might be blotted out of the Book of Life in an instant if I didn't toe the line.

So, toe I did. With the exception of holding hands with a boy at a few varsity basketball games, I was winning at both school and church, all the while remaining relatively well-liked by my class of fifty-two students. Still, just for good measure, I'd re-ask Jesus into my heart a few times a week—a sort of insurance policy against my constant fear that He would turn His back on me if I didn't hold up my end of the deal.

WRIST CORSAGES AND MOZZARELLA STICKS

High school began in all its glory with braces, classes in a new wing of the school, and banquets instead of dances (because that was how we liked things at our tiny Christian school). Valentine's Day was just around the corner and who-was-asking-whom to the Valentine's Banquet was the talk of the ninth grade.

Word had a way of traveling fast in a class of our size, and more than one friend warned me that a certain guy had plans to ask me to the banquet.

Now, fourteen-year-old Raechel was good at a lot of things, but disappointing people was not one of them. This boy was a great kid, but I didn't know him very well and the thought of attending my first-ever high school banquet with him made me super nervous.

I knew I needed a plan, and I needed one fast. So, just after fourth period, I raced to the boys' lockers (Yes, there was a boys' side of the hall. I know.) to find Ryan "Blue Eyes" Myers putting his books away. Ninth-Grade Ryan was quite a bit taller than First-Grade Ryan, but that wasn't the only thing that had changed. He was still . . . energetic . . . but by now he was also working his way to handsome and he was my very best guy friend.

"Quick! Ask me to the Valentine's Banquet!" I blurted breathlessly as I nearly knocked him into his locker with urgency.

"Um . . . would you like to go to the Valentine's Banquet with me?" he answered hesitantly, the way adolescent boys do when they are mauled at their lockers by overly-aggressive girl friends.

At the moment, it was a simple solution to a high-school-sized problem. But in fact, this was the sealed-for-the-history-books moment Ryan "Blue Eyes" Myers asked me on our first date.

Super intentional. Super romantic.

I'll spare you the details of the blessed evening, but some highlights included my Aunt Sheri as our minivan chauffeur, a wrist corsage the size of my face, mozzarella sticks in the corner booth at Applebee's with our friends, and let us never forget my braces and my impossible-to-walk-in, first pair of high heels.

Some first dates are all sparks and sizzle, but ours was more lasagna and quiet clapping while the junior high principal did stand-up in the school cafeteria. Romance was not in the air. Ryan was a friend who said yes to another friend. Still, our most-awkward, least-romantic first date was important because I felt seen and special and safe, which was exactly what my high school freshman heart needed.

BETWEEN TOLEDO AND ORLANDO

This was growing up for me. Life verses were less of a thing back then, but if I'd had one, it probably would have been Ephesians 4:30, "Do not grieve the Holy Spirit" (ESV) or just the middle part of James 2:18, "You have faith and I have works."

I was driven to be good. Determined to find myself approved by anyone and everyone who knew me. And I pulled it off pretty well. I was a leader in my school and in my youth group. All of the kids at church occupied the back three pews most Sunday mornings until I convinced everyone to move to the front three. I graciously showed the public school kids how to take notes, and our beloved pastor got more eye contact from me than anyone else in the youth group.

In high school theology class we memorized the Westminster Shorter Catechism, exegeted Scripture, and by the time our pastor was on the second point of any given three-point sermon, I was certain I could have taken the pulpit and finished the third point with him.

A month before graduation, we took a senior class trip to Florida, and I was randomly selected to take a shift riding shotgun with the bus driver overnight while the rest of the class slept. As we barreled down the highway somewhere between Toledo and Orlando, the bus driver, Bill, asked me about my plans after graduation. I flapped my adorable jaw about how I knew everything there was to know about God and the Bible by now. I really wanted to go to interior design school, and after twelve years of private Christian education, I saw no need for further study of Scripture or spiritual instruction. It was the end of my senior year, and I was ready to graduate Christianity with a fully sanctified scholarship in life.

My soul had no need for a Savior, or so it seemed. After all, I assumed I had done the saving through years of right answers and right behavior. I had worked hard for approval and succeeded, trusting my goodness to save me.

I had nailed it and thoroughly missed it all at once, all the while living in complete and devastating darkness. I checked and re-checked the "saved" box, just to make sure, knowing nothing of true salvation by grace through faith.

That night, Bill didn't tell me all the hundred ways I'd gotten it wrong or laugh me off the bus. It was worse than that—*he wasn't impressed by me.* In the honesty of that moment, just two people and a whole lot of highway, all the words I'd served him didn't return the usual, "Wow, you're such a great kid!" Instead, he looked concerned. This was new and puzzling for the good girl accustomed to good reviews.

The conversation grew quiet after that. I pretended I was tired, so we rode on through the rest of my shotgun shift in silence. The yellow lines and the lights from the other cars whizzed past in the other direction while I sat, wondering what on earth I was missing. God was at work in my "good," dark heart, revealing a need for Him I'd honestly never noticed before.

PLUS NOTHING

I spent the first eighteen years of my life believing a diminished gospel. I believed my salvation was a combination of Christ's work on the cross and my effort in life. We (Jesus and I) would work in tandem to save me. And any time I did something to jeopardize the work He did, I'd promise I could do even better next time if that was what it took.

I was a tidy little mess. A little bit self-absorbed (I was the "pretty one," after all), but overall a homecoming court, student government, varsity volleyball, cutest couple, model citizen.

How could Jesus *not* love me?

I was living and breathing and putting all my eggs in the basket of an almost-gospel. A watered-down, diminished gospel that was really no gospel at all.

Then I went to college.

I'll be the first to admit my college experience wasn't typical. Sure, I was experiencing freshman dorm life at a four-year, liberal arts Christian college. But my life looked very different from the other girls on my floor.

Ryan and I had officially begun dating when we were sixteen years old (almost exactly a year after the Valentine's Banquet). By the time we went to college, we'd known each other for twelve years and dated for three. With so much life together behind us, we must have seemed like an old married couple compared to our friends and their always-dramatic, tenderly new relationships.

Freshmen in college, barely out from under our parents' roofs, Ryan and I were ready to talk marriage.

We knew we wanted to be married, but we wanted to go about it properly. We sought counsel from our parents, from the college chaplain, and from the pastors of our churches back home and at school. Not long after Ryan popped the question during a visit to our favorite fountain in downtown Chicago, Blue Eyes and I enrolled ourselves in premarital counseling.

Every Tuesday evening, after classes and homework, Ryan would pick me up at my dorm and we'd drive to the church for an hour of marriage prep. Thursday nights we'd drive the same route to join the men's and women's Bible studies, where most of the other men and women were easily double or triple our age. We really wanted to get this right, so we did everything we could think to do, even if we were the only kids our age doing it.

First, premarital counseling is a must. It's hilarious and heated and awkward and critical all at once, and you absolutely must do it. Our pastor's wife led us in all but one of ten sessions. The one night we talked about sex, she asked another woman from the church to step in because she absolutely could not look anyone in the eye if the word "sex" was floating around in the air. Could not. If we even entered the vicinity of that marriage topic during the other weeks, her face would flush and conversation would be quickly diverted before things got carried away.

(Bless premarital counseling, you guys. And the people who care enough to give their evenings to loving young couples, often asking nothing in return. Even if one of the best parts of marriage gets the taboo buzzer 90 percent of the time, it was still so worth it.)

Second, those Bible studies were something else. Honestly, they were a gift, but not for reasons you might expect. Our Thursday night drives back to campus had us asking more questions about what God's Word did and didn't say than we'd ever asked in our lives. We were becoming adults. Our faith was becoming our own. And when dots weren't connecting, we dug until they did.

Those Thursday nights are when I learned about grace. Not because it was being taught at our Bible Study, but precisely because it wasn't. As we went to church and wrote our papers in school, we began to suspect something was missing. And if not, would we really spend the rest of our lives making up for where the cross of Jesus left off?

Ryan and I began to dig deep into our Bibles together, really for the very first time. We started to ask questions outside of our church and college campus relationships. Through the work of the Holy Spirit, as well as my sister and a few other mentors, we were shocked and relieved to find that we had nothing to contribute to the saving of our souls.

When I was twenty years old, God showed me a salvation that didn't need me. I learned that right behavior for the wrong reasons is not what God requires of me. I had tried for a decade to justify myself by works, meeting Jesus halfway, combining our efforts to complete the job:

Christ died for me *plus* I'm keeping myself pure for marriage.

Christ died for me *plus* I don't drink, smoke, or chew, or go with boys who do.

Christ died for me *plus* I give my tithe to the church.

I watched as my college friends did the same. We struggled through a gospel of not enough. We weren't enough for God, and Christ's sacrifice wasn't enough to set us free. We were enslaved and judgey all at the same time, looking down our noses at the other girls whose lives weren't all buttoned up, but feeling trapped on the treadmill of effort for everlasting life.

Thanks be to God, grace set me free. The moment I finally understood I couldn't save myself was the day I began living because of what Jesus did, not because of what I needed to convince Him to do.

Christ died for me. Plus nothing.

Moving forward, my life may not have looked much different on the outside—I still lived what looked like a Christian life. But this time, it really was one. With a heart of gratitude, I walked in the fullness of a gospel that invited me instead of needed me.

INVITED TO SOMETHING NEW

I wish I could say I don't struggle with legalism as much anymore. I still act to save myself sometimes. I probably always will. I still find myself opening my Bible because I ought to and not because I get to. I still find myself refraining from offensive language because I don't want to get in trouble or offend, not because I want to honor the Lord with my heart and my words. I still sometimes forget that the work of Christ was complete when He breathed "It is finished" from the cross, and any gospel that distracts from, or adds to, or takes away from that is false.

Maybe legalism isn't your struggle but grace abuse is. As much as I'm still tempted to believe what I do saves me, I sometimes also find myself on the opposite side of the street, treating grace like a get-out-of-jail-free card. *It doesn't matter how I live because grace covers it all!* I'm guilty of grace-guzzling to the point of abuse, acting outside of what the Bible prescribes for Christian living because, *Hey, it's not my works that save me anyway!*

The truth is, anything that diminishes or dishonors the work of Christ on the cross is a false gospel. It's the gospel Paul wrote feverishly against in chains as he defended the truest Truth of what Christ had done, just a generation before he lived.

In Romans 6:1–11, Paul asks me (yep, I'm pretty sure he's talking right at me), "What should we say then? Should we continue in sin so that grace may multiply? Absolutely not! How can we who died to sin still live in it?" As he continues, Paul invites us to something new. "Just as Christ was raised from the dead by the glory of the Father, so we too may walk in a new way of life. . . . For we know that our old self was crucified with Him in order that sin's dominion over the body may be abolished, so that we may no longer be enslaved to sin, since a person who has died is freed from sin's claims." And just as quickly as He reins us in from grace-abuse, He frees us to live in Christ, "For in light of the fact that He died, He died to sin once for all; but in light of the fact that He lives, He lives to God. So, you too consider yourselves dead to sin but alive to God in Christ Jesus."

Alive to God, indeed. As Ryan and I married a year and a half later on my aunt and uncle's lawn in southeast Michigan, we recessed down the aisle both in need and in full supply of Christ's finished work. Whatever life brought our newlywed way, we were grateful to know we'd be walking forward with a Savior who never gave up on us, and who we trusted would never leave us.

SO CLOSE, YET SO FAR AWAY

Last Christmas I made an epic mistake.

In an attempt to do something thoughtful and festive for my family, I purchased four really excellent seats to see the Rockettes in the Radio City Christmas Spectacular. Ryan and I hadn't been in a decade, and the show is always so entertaining. I had found a coupon online, but it was still a splurge.

Just after checking out, I closed my laptop, satisfied and excited. This would be an awesome surprise—we were going to have so much fun!

I was dying to tell someone my secret, so when I bumped into my friend Kaitlin a few minutes later, I told her about the tickets.

"So fun! I didn't know the Rockettes were in Nashville this year," she replied. "Where are they performing?"

"Yep, they are! They'll be at Radio City."

[awkward pause]

"Rae, Radio City is in New York."

"No, it's not. Nashville is called 'Radio City.'"

This, of course, is when it hit me. I'm not sure if I was more red from embarrassment or white from panic. Nashville is called *Music* City, and I had just purchased four very expensive tickets for my family to see the Rockettes. In New York. Next week.

Flights to New York would have escalated this special splurge to a budget-busting binge, so I immediately got on the phone with Ticketmaster to explain my very unfortunate mistake.

"You must think I am so foolish," I said to the woman on the other end of the line as she graciously cancelled my order and refunded my money.

"Oh honey, you'd be surprised. Just before you called, I gave a man a refund because his wife accidentally bought them tickets to see the 'Red Hot Chili Pipers.'"

We laughed hard together and imagined how many other couples may have made the same mistake and would inevitably exchange frustrated words upon arrival at the bagpipe concert. *You had one job!*

That day I learned an important lesson. Even though they may sound similar, Radio City is not the same as Music City, and the Red Hot Chili Pipers are not "close enough" to the Red Hot Chili Peppers. Getting something almost right can still be incredibly wrong.

TRUTH-ADJACENT

Remember when we sat around my living room together back in chapter 1? (Metaphorically, of course. I wish it were in person!) We looked down into our cups to find the truth of our present circumstances. Then, looking up from the good/bad/wonderful/horrible truth in front of us, we set our eyes on the truer, permanent Truth of God's steadfast faithfulness.

Sometimes, though, we look up from our cups and stop short of the truest Truth.

My young cup was full of the shock of my parents' divorce, failed attempts to get my father to truly see me, and an exhausting effort to control what I could, to be approved of and loved.

So, looking up, I set my gaze on achievement, on making a better life for myself by making *me* better for everyone else. Even when my cup was filled with success or friendship or love, it took me a long time to look up from the truth in my cup to the truest Truth of the cross. I did good things, sometimes even for good reasons. I pursued what masqueraded convincingly as Truth, but until I knew I needed Jesus, it was still only ever truth-adjacent.

We're adults now, most of us. But that doesn't make it any easier to discern Truth from truth-adjacent. Sometimes the results are fixable and make for a good story, like thinking Nashville was called Radio City, but often the consequences have much higher stakes.

Paul warned Timothy two thousand years ago that "the time will come when [the Church] will not tolerate sound doctrine, but according to their own desires, will multiply teachers for themselves because they have an itch to hear something new. They will turn away from hearing the truth and will turn aside to myths" (2 Tim. 4:3–4).

Paul knew truth-adjacent would be appealing. Even now we want new teachers and fresh truths—we want a gospel that depends on us, at least a little. But just like Kaitlin alerted me to my festive holiday error, Paul wasn't afraid to raise the false gospel red flag any time the Church fell short of Truth. And, neither should we.

Truth-adjacent is everywhere. Something may sound and even look a lot like Truth. But Paul warned us then and we get to remind each other now: if we are hanging our hat on something that points us away from our need for Jesus, it is not true.

Salvation because we're walking the line is gospel-adjacent.

Salvation because we cannot do what Christ has done is gospel.

Peace because we've stripped back our busyness, simplified our schedules, and picked our yeses and nos carefully is truth-adjacent.

Peace because God's Word is an anchor for our souls no matter how simple or messy our lives look is Truth.

This. THIS is why we read Truth.

We've been offered false gospels and taught truth-adjacencies by some of the most well-meaning men and women we'll ever know. But we read God's Word to find the Truth. We study and know and memorize God's Word because we cannot waste any more of our precious time on this earth believing the lies. Even the lies that sound really good and entertaining and close enough.

God's Word is truer and more lasting than the truth-adjacent theories the world will try to sell you. Whether we honestly struggle to "remember whose we are," or successfully satisfy an almost-gospel, both situations find us equally and desperately in need of Christ's finished work on the cross.

God the Father did not send His Son so that I would spend my childhood striving to be a blue-ribbon daughter.

Jesus didn't live a sinless life so that we could be ever reminded of our shortcomings.

Christ did not die for truth-adjacent. And the sooner we insist on Truth exactly, the gospel plus nothing, and refuse to settle on anything less, the sooner we start living lives of simple, thankful service to our all-sufficient Savior.

SHE READS TRUTH

ROMANS 6:1–14 ESV

What shall we say then? Are we to continue in sin that grace may abound? By no means! How can we who died to sin still live in it? Do you not know that all of us who have been baptized into Christ Jesus were baptized into his death? We were buried therefore with him by baptism into death, in order that, just as Christ was raised from the dead by the glory of the Father, we too might walk in newness of life.

For if we have been united with him in a death like his, we shall certainly be united with him in a resurrection like his. We know that our old self was crucified with him in order that the body of sin might be brought to nothing, so that we would no longer be enslaved to sin. For one who has died has been set free from sin. Now if we have died with Christ, we believe that we will also live with him. We know that Christ, being raised from the dead, will never die again; death no longer has dominion over him. For the death he died he died to sin, once for all, but the life he lives he lives to God. So you also must consider yourselves dead to sin and alive to God in Christ Jesus.

Let not sin therefore reign in your mortal body, to make you obey its passions. Do not present your members to sin as instruments for unrighteousness, but present yourselves to God as those who have been brought from death to life, and your members to God as instruments for righteousness. For sin will have no dominion over you, since you are not under law but under grace.

2 TIMOTHY 4:1-8 ESV

I charge you in the presence of God and of Christ Jesus, who is to judge the living and the dead, and by his appearing and his kingdom: preach the word; be ready in season and out of season; reprove, rebuke, and exhort, with complete patience and teaching. For the time is coming when people will not endure sound teaching, but having itching ears they will accumulate for themselves teachers to suit their own passions, and will turn away from listening to the truth and wander off into myths. As for you, always be sober-minded, endure suffering, do the work of an evangelist, fulfill your ministry.

For I am already being poured out as a drink offering, and the time of my departure has come. I have fought the good fight, I have finished the race, I have kept the faith. Henceforth there is laid up for me the crown of righteousness, which the Lord, the righteous judge, will award to me on that Day, and not only to me but also to all who have loved his appearing.

EXQUISITE MERCY

God's Mercy Is Permanent
Even When Our Bodies Pass Away

A *bba, Father! All things are possible for You. Take this cup away from me. Nevertheless, not what I will, but what You will"* (Mark 14:36).

I prayed desperately as I soaked in the bathtub, the room lit only by the moon. My hands circled my eight-months-round belly while sobs quieted to a steady stream of unnoticed tears falling to join the bathwater.

She hadn't moved in twelve hours. A hundred things could have explained it away, but my mother's heart knew what it refused to say out loud: our baby girl had left us. She wasn't in there anymore.

I knew what I didn't want to know. What I didn't want to be true. What they told us was coming any day for the last eleven weeks, but we hoped would never come.

I soaked and prayed. My mind went back and forth between preparing for what the days ahead would hold, and begging the Lord for an escape route from this path of sorrow I knew tomorrow would bring.

The sun would rise soon. Ready or not. And when Ryan woke up, he would have to know what I knew. I would have to break his heart with mine. Locked into a roller coaster with no emergency exit, the car was clicking ahead toward the most treacherous drop of our lives.

As the sun rose across our backyard, Ryan found me on the sofa in the living room, drifted off in prayer and sadness and exhaustion. My husband and her daddy, he already knew, too.

Then scenes flash. Calling my Bible study group to tell them our girl was in heaven. Packing a bag for a hospital trip I didn't want to take. Kissing our toddler son goodbye. Stopping for a jacket on the way out the front door, gripped by the reality that she wouldn't be coming back with us. The next time I would stand in that foyer, I would be emptied.

Silence as my midwife placed the ultrasound wand on my belly. A nod. Alone in the room, I crawled into Ryan's lap and he cradled me and we wept in silence for a long time.

I felt alone. Just one person again, not two.

Another flash of another screen at the hospital. Her still body and another nod. Hello and good-bye were coming, and they'd come together.

Father, please take this cup from me.

Two hearts being monitored on the screen. One flat-lined, the other heartbroken.

In and out of sleep and prayer and a visit with our pastor and the promise of heaven and perfect knowledge. Walking through hell with the hope of heaven.

In and out of day and night, the inevitable came. It was time and we would never be ready. Nothing would ever be as unnatural as pushing a child out of my body and into the grave.

This was not hello. Birth was good-bye.

With Ryan at my side, she arrives, and as we lay our parent-eyes on our still daughter, we hold her close and whisper through tears.

Hello.

We love you.

We want you.

You look like your brother, and you have your mom's mouth.

Facing the impossible task of cramming a lifetime of love and parenthood into ninety torn minutes, we talk to our daughter, sing to her, pray thanks for her. We study her small body from head to toe in aching awe of how mysteriously and wonderfully she was made.

A deficit of oxygen in the room made up for with a surplus of peace.

We want you. We want more of you.

We weigh her. We love her more than two pounds, four ounces of anything else on the face of this earth. Ninety minutes to be her mother. Kisses, care, bunting, sharing, caressing. Holding her as close as we can get, knowing she is already gone.

Good-bye, little one.

Just as quickly as she came, she is gone. I can't think about where or with whom. To imagine my baby in the hands of strangers invites more intense panic than a mother's body is made to endure.

Are they looking at her with kind eyes?

Is she warm enough?

Is she . . .

I can't. My heart cannot.

The sounds of grief that came from our own bodies that day were unrecognizable—like they came from someone else. Wheeled to recover past the rooms of new parents, balloons, and exhausted bliss. New moms aren't supposed to sleep through the night. And when their milk comes in, there should be someone to relieve them—someone to need it.

Back home to empty the very next day. Body empty. Arms empty. Eyes empty. Maternity clothes put away and everything back to normal. At the park the next week, kids played and moms chatted and I wanted to scream.

She was here. She was real. I promise.

And we wanted her.

And now she's in the ground across town and not here with me.

But she was—she was here just a couple of days ago.

No one else's world had stopped while ours had imploded. I was angry and hurting. It didn't seem fair. The cup did not pass from us. The only way out was onward, drinking deeply. Honoring our daughter and her Maker with our grief for a life lost.

Not my will, but Yours be done.

They were the safest, most dangerous words we have ever spoken. They terrified us. Putting our lives and the life of our daughter in the hands of the One who gives and takes away.

We gave her to Him. And He took her.

And we gave thanks.

IN THE GARDEN

On the night Jesus was betrayed, Scripture tells us He was "deeply distressed and horrified" and His soul was "swallowed up in sorrow" (Mark 14:33–34). He knew what was coming. Both fully God and fully man, Jesus didn't have the luxury of wondering how the next twenty-four hours would unfold. He knew.

He would never sleep again.

He would be dead by this time tomorrow.

The pain of personal betrayals would be matched only by the graphic violence of His own flesh being raked, and torn, and beaten.

He knew and He was horrified and He prayed a "yes" to His Father because of His love for us.

"Abba, Father! All things are possible for You. Take this cup away from Me. Nevertheless, not what I will, but what You will" (Mark 14:36).

As Christ wrestled—even as He said "yes"—He also asked for escape.

I take great comfort knowing I'm not the first to have prayed this prayer—to know I'm not wrong to ask for relief. Jesus went first. He gave us permission to ask to be relieved of our burdens and our sorrows. He also showed us how to trust the Father when He asks us to drink deeply from the cup He has given us (Heb. 5:7).

The Father did not take the cup of suffering from Him. The suffering came—just moments after Jesus' prayer, Scripture says, "The hour [was] at hand" (Matt. 26:45 ESV). An act of severe mercy. Only this mercy wasn't for the object of the suffering; it was for you and me. It was our mercy.

Our exquisite mercy.

Because Jesus said yes in the garden—and only because of this—we can say yes to whatever we find in our own cups. Severe or spectacular, we can drink in obedience knowing the only One with the authority to put anything in our cup is the Father Himself. And just as He has the power to fill our cups with bitter and sweet things, He also has the power to take them away if we ask. He invites us to ask.

NOT MY WILL, BUT YOURS

From the afternoon of our routine twenty-week ultrasound, when a healthy pregnancy turned into a parent's worst nightmare, we prayed.

You have overcome the world.

Take this cup from us.

Not our will, but Yours.

Our truth was one thing for so long. My belly was growing. My cravings were adorably obnoxious. Our son was going to be a big brother and we were bracing for life as parents of two kids under the age of two.

This real-life truth changed in an instant the day the doctors discovered fluid on our baby's brain, a hypoplastic left side of her heart, and ultimately an extra ninth chromosome. Normal would never be the same. Not for us.

"Not compatible with life," they said.

"Could be any day; pay attention to her movements," they cautioned.

"Call us when the time comes," they offered when there was nothing left to say.

Our permanent had passed away in an afternoon.

Everything still looked exactly the same. My belly continued to grow. Cashiers at the grocery store still congratulated me. Friends who hadn't heard our diagnosis asked how nursery decorating was coming along.

One afternoon, a few weeks into our painful new permanent, I asked my mom to take me shopping for a bonnet for our girl. Even if we didn't get to keep her, I wanted to be her mom. In my sorrow, the best way I could think to do that was to buy my daughter a bonnet. While we browsed, a well-meaning clerk offered the prettiest bonnet in the store, acknowledging its high price, but pointing out its heirloom potential. "Your daughter can wear this as a baby, then carry it as a handkerchief on her wedding day!"

Lord, I prayed that night, *heal her. Please. Take this cup from us.*

But not my will. Let Your will be done in my daughter's life.

Weeks passed, and the reality of this cup continued to turn our truth upside down. One afternoon, I lay on my bed to read while our son napped. The Bible resting on my belly began to bounce while my baby girl kicked and punched and turned just beneath my skin. Unable to live apart from me, but very much alive inside of me.

This was my new truth. My womb was a place of life, but it would soon become a place of death.

Waking up every morning was like pulling the trigger in a game of Russian roulette. *Will today be a click or a bang?* Opening my eyes from sleep, I'd hold my hand to my belly and wait for signs of life. *Is she still there? Will today be good-bye?*

Eleven weeks we waited for the trigger to catch. We didn't make plans. Our only certainty was that life was fragile and everything could and would change in an instant.

In a fog, we found we could see only one thing clearly: nothing was certain but what God promised in His Word. Nothing was true but His Truth. Waking up every morning was a gamble, but God was faithful. He hadn't changed. In my twenty-six years, it was the first time I ever really understood how singularly reliable God's Word really was.

Seventy-seven nights I fell asleep waiting for death to come. Some nights I'd wake up to the sound of my own voice quoting Scripture.

Satan comes to kill, steal, and destroy.

Death is a thief.

Satan is a thief.

Or I'd recall passages I memorized as a child as I drifted into sleep:

Now we see but a poor reflection as in a mirror; then we shall see face to face. Now I know in part; then I shall know fully, even as I am fully known.

Waking and sleeping, God's Word was there. It was the one sure thing I knew would not disappear.

Some nights I'd wake up sweating from dreams of babies missing or falling—sometimes actually leaping across the bed to catch phantom infants before they fell or rolled away from me.

In one particularly vivid dream, Ryan and I were standing on the beach and the sky was beautiful. Then, out of nowhere, the sky grew dark with a tidal wave as high as the sky in the distance, coming our way.

There was a large wall of rock on the shore with many crevices and pockets. Ryan told me to hold tight; the tidal wave would hit any minute and this was our only shot at survival. We buried our faces into the rock just as the wave crashed, slamming our bodies so hard we almost lost our grip. More waves came that threatened our grip and we found pockets of air in the rock and did not drown.

I recorded this dream in a pink hardcover journal a friend sent me when she heard our news. Looking at it now, the writing almost illegible and the pages smeared with tears, I remember the true torment as I wrote, bracing for the real-life tidal wave that would soon reach our family's shore. I didn't know then the way I understand now that the steadfastness of God and His Word would save our family, just like the rock we white-knuckled in my dream saved us from drowning.

Seventy-seven nights I fell asleep waiting for death to come. And seventy-seven mornings I woke, relieved to find evidence of life. On the 78th day—on April 7, 2008—our Evie Grace gave me one strong kick up high in my belly and I made note of the time in my head: 1 p.m.

Good kick, baby girl! You are so strong!

That kick was the last sign of life we would get from our girl.

That night I paced while Ryan was away at a church event. I called my sister and told her I was afraid. And when Ryan came home, he prayed over me for wisdom, peace, and Presence. We spoke with our midwife on the phone and decided to see what the morning brought.

Maybe it was nothing.

Everyone was asleep and we didn't want to bother them.

The midwife said to call back in the morning.

We went to bed and tried to get some rest. Just as soon as Ryan fell asleep, I crept into our bathroom, turned on the bathwater, and prayed like Jesus prayed in Gethsemane before His arrest:

Father, take this cup from me.

I prayed with faith that an escape route was possible. And I prayed with trust that the Lord cared for me and for my family. I didn't know what would happen to us, but I knew that I knew that I knew that God was faithful.

Not my will, but Yours, Lord.

THE SAME AMOUNT OF FAITHFUL

Maybe you're familiar with this chaos of nothing certain. Maybe you've gone to bed not knowing what the next morning will bring, checking for signs of life the moment you wake up. A pregnancy or a child, a spouse or a friend; perhaps a relationship on life support.

You've been given a particularly bitter cup and you've asked the Lord to take it from you, asking yourself if you're willing to drink it to the dregs if that is what He asks of you.

You've wanted to run, but known drinking from the cup in the Lord's presence is better than escape. You lean in, knowing it will be the most difficult season of your life, like a tidal wave growing to slam you into the Rock. You know this suffering may save you.

Maybe you, like me, have learned over time to name this bitter cup Mercy.

Mercy was present as my first permanent thing passed away at the age of seven. My family was never the same, but God was at work.

Mercy was there as I navigated childhood with one parent in prison and as my dad's new family happened in front of me. God was at work then, too.

Mercy sat with us in the waiting room that January afternoon in 2008 as we stood on the beach of calm waters, not knowing our sky would grow dark on the other side of the exam room door.

And Mercy was there when we groaned goodbyes to our little girl's earthly body and returned home to a new, unwelcomed permanent.

It is God's exquisite mercy that asks us to drink the cup of suffering. As we drink, with only our present circumstances in view, God is right there, faithful and at work, with all of eternity in view.

Allowing us to be pressed, but protecting us from being crushed.

Permitting persecution, but never abandoning.

Striking us down, but not destroying us (2 Cor. 4:8–9).

Every day seems more fragile than the next. Every new wave slams into us, threatening to shake us loose, but because the Rock doesn't move, neither do we. The Truth of God's Word echoes in our ears and we go to sleep at night knowing whatever tomorrow holds—life or death or things present or things to come—nothing "will have the power to separate us from the love of God that is in Christ Jesus our Lord!" (Rom. 8:39).

Our truth was the stillbirth of our daughter to Trisomy 9 when I was thirty-two weeks pregnant. Our truest Truth was that God was exactly the same amount of faithful then as He was when our son Oliver was born healthy two years earlier. And when our daughter Hazel was born healthy two years later.

God was just as faithful then as He was when He taught us about His grace as newlywed college students—and when He promised to make Abraham into a great nation, and to be Israel's God because they would be His people.

No more. No less.

While everything else in our world changed, the Truth we found in God's Word did not change. He did not change.

From the foundation of the world, one thing Did. Not. Change.

Our cup may be filled with something completely different tomorrow than it is today. Much to our chagrin, God is not bound by our planners. And so tonight, before we close our eyes, we pray and scribble across the pages of our agendas: Not my will, but Yours.

When we rise, we give thanks for whatever we find in our cup. We call it mercy—exquisite mercy. And because we read Truth, we know:

Nothing can separate us from Christ (Rom. 8:38–39).

Even if we pass through the fire, we will not be burned (Isa. 43:2).

The waves will not overcome us (Isa. 43:2).

And we know His power is made perfect in our weakness (2 Cor. 12:9).

We have learned to trust the One who fills our cups with sweet and bitter things. We know He may take the cup away, and He may ask us to drink it to the dregs, but He will never not be faithful.

DO NOT FORSAKE THE WORK OF YOUR HANDS

I put off visiting Evie's gravesite for three months after we buried her.

Only a parent who has turned through the pages of a headstone catalog can understand how sacred that ground is. Too sacred to approach most days. Too cruel to trod. Knowing your child is in the ground beneath you makes every maternal instinct you've ever had fire on all cylinders, and it takes superhuman willpower, and sometimes a strong friend, to keep you from just digging.

Three months is a long time to wait, but that was how long it took for me.

One Wednesday afternoon in July, without warning, it had been exactly long enough. Suddenly, I needed to be where she was, no matter how much it hurt. I grabbed my Bible, my tennis shoes, and my courage and drove in the direction of my baby.

With no headstone yet, I knew our girl's place by the small white cross her daddy had laid on the overturned dirt before we left her that day in April. It was still there. Which meant she was still there. Simultaneously comforting and crushing.

As I sat in the dirt next to my daughter's grave, I talked to her. I don't have any idea what people do at gravesites, but it felt nice to greet her and to let her know that we were doing alright. I had my Bible tucked under my arm. I didn't have a plan, but I knew I was definitely going to want it.

It felt appropriate to read a psalm, so I opened my Bible and it fell naturally open to Psalm 139. I'd spent a lot of time camped out in the Truth of that page over the past six months, but I was hungry for God to show me something new. Psalm 138 was one page over, so I began to read it aloud—maybe to myself, maybe to my daughter, maybe just to prove I was still breathing:

I give you thanks, O Lord, with my whole heart;

As I inhaled and exhaled, I prayed the words I was reading:

On the day I called, you answered me;
my strength of soul you increased.

It was the Truth. He had always answered me. But would I ever feel whole again?

Though I walk in the midst of trouble,
you preserve my life;
you stretch out your hand against the wrath of my enemies,
and your right hand delivers me.

Yes, God had delivered me, but did that mean my story was over? Would this be the one great work of God in my life? Was this His singular effort to call me to Himself and to mold me?

The Lord will fulfill his purpose for me;
your steadfast love, O Lord, endures forever.
Do not forsake the work of your hands.

I realized as I read that last portion of Psalm 138 in the dirt that day that the Lord was doing a greater work in me. My own flesh and blood had passed away, but this tragedy wasn't the end of my story, and it wasn't the only part of my story. It was a piece, and more pieces would come. More victories. More sorrows.

Just as I prayed "not my will, but Yours" over my daughter's fading life, I was learning to trust my own life to the long-game God—the God who *will* fulfill His purpose for me, not who already *has*.

And so, even eight years after that July afternoon, sitting in the soil at the site of my daughter's grave, I continue to pray with the psalmist, believing,

> The LORD will fulfill His purpose for me.
> LORD, Your love is eternal;
> do not abandon the work of Your hands. (Ps. 138:8)

SHE READS TRUTH

2 CORINTHIANS 4:7-12, 16-18 ESV

But we have this treasure in jars of clay, to show that the surpassing power belongs to God and not to us. We are afflicted in every way, but not crushed; perplexed, but not driven to despair; persecuted, but not forsaken; struck down, but not destroyed; always carrying in the body the death of Jesus, so that the life of Jesus may also be manifested in our bodies. For we who live are always being given over to death for Jesus' sake, so that the life of Jesus also may be manifested in our mortal flesh. So death is at work in us, but life in you. . . .

So we do not lose heart. Though our outer self is wasting away, our inner self is being renewed day by day. For this light momentary affliction is preparing for us an eternal weight of glory beyond all comparison, as we look not to the things that are seen but to the things that are unseen. For the things that are seen are transient, but the things that are unseen are eternal.

FRESH OUT OF HOPE

God's Hope Is Permanent
When Our Plans Are Passing Away

I'm all out of hope."

They were the only words my broken and fearful heart could mutter as I rocked in the chair on Katie's front porch that June afternoon.

Katie was my most Southern friend. She not only had white rocking chairs on her front porch, she used them often—rocking slowly while drinking sweet tea, using phrases like "fixin' to," and waving her University of Tennessee flag every weekend of college football season.

Her lush, well-watered ferns hung at intervals between white porch posts, offering shade and hospitality while we rocked. I studied their greenness and fullness and remembered my own porch ferns just one street over, dried up and stringy.

The ferns were appropriately reflective of what was happening inside our home. We were parched. We'd been grieving for fourteen months, the pain piling on as we lost two more early pregnancies that fall and winter. Life was constant triage—like being in surgery for still-fresh wounds, incurring new traumas before we could stitch up the last ones.

Ryan and I had given everything we had to pursue our big plan of a big family, but by this point, it looked like we may only ever be a family of three. It was taking all of our focus to submit to this new reality.

Getting pregnant wasn't the issue for us, though I know it's a struggle for many. We'd celebrated the thrill of six positive pregnancy tests between the fall of 2005 and the spring of 2009. I remember doing the math: 102 total weeks of pregnancy, and only one child at our breakfast table in the mornings. No, getting pregnant wasn't the problem. The problem was that getting pregnant was no longer good news. It was terrifying.

Two pink lines meant loss was imminent, or at least inevitable. It meant it was time to brace our hearts and minds and marriage for grief on repeat. Everything about pregnancy and childbirth was stained with fear and trauma, so we decided it was time to do more than stop trying—it was time to start trying to keep this from happening ever again. We'd done so well taking turns in our grief after we lost Evie. But I was spiraling, and there was no more see to my saw. I was down for the count and Ryan could see I was slipping away.

People told us not to lose hope, and we hadn't. But we had a new, less optimistic perspective on hope. We believed with all our hearts that we could hope to eternity and back in God's promises. We also knew (because we checked for ourselves) that God never promised us another healthy baby. The Bible promises a lot of things—it even promised babies to a handful of super unlikely candidates for motherhood—and all of those promises are take-to-the-bank true. But we can't hope for things that aren't promised . . . right?

We can hope in a new heaven and new earth because God promises those things will be ours one day (Isa. 65:17).

We can hope in an imperishable, unfading salvation because God's Word says it is kept in heaven for us (1 Pet. 1:4).

We can hope death will come to an end, and that the Thief will be defeated once and for all. God promised that, too (Rev. 21:4; Rom. 16:20).

We have all kinds of hope because Jesus promised all in one breath that we will have trouble, but that He has already overcome the world (John 16:33).

But in fourteen months of grieving and searching, I found no promise regarding the expansion of our future family—no guarantee that God would give me a healthy pregnancy. My weary heart was only interested in hoping for things I knew were going to happen. And so, in spite of all of the high-hopers around me, I was unwilling to play games of false or unfounded hope.

A STUDY IN CONTENTMENT

A month before I found myself on Katie's very-Southern front porch, rocking and not hoping, we had already made the decision to move on with our lives. We packed up our baby clothes and equipment and distributed them among my fertile and fortunate friends. In exchange, I purchased a small book about contentment, which mainly pointed me to the book of Philippians.

I was determined to align myself with the Lord in the way the apostle Paul modeled. He had found the secret to being content in any and every situation, after all, and I needed to know that secret.

For a week, I studied Paul's letter from prison to the Philippians— chapter 4, especially. If he could write with joy in chains, I could raise my two-year-old with joy while grieving in Franklin, Tennessee.

From his prison cell, Paul wrote:

> Rejoice in the Lord always. I will say it again: Rejoice! Let your graciousness be known to everyone. The Lord is near. Don't worry about anything, but in everything, through prayer and petition with thanksgiving, let your requests be made known to God. And the peace of God, which surpasses every thought, will guard your hearts and minds in Christ Jesus. (Phil. 4:4–7)

I was learning. *I can pray for the things I want, and hope in things I know are true.* The only trouble was, I didn't know what to pray for anymore.

So I prayed, "I think I just need You, Lord. That's all I know to want. Can I trust You to be the guard of my heart and mind?"

And Paul kept on writing while his chains clinked:

> Finally brothers, whatever is true, whatever is honorable, whatever is just, whatever is pure, whatever is lovely, whatever is commendable—if there is any moral excellence and if there is any praise—dwell on these things. Do what you have learned and received and heard and seen in me, and the God of peace will be with you. (vv. 8–9)

Paul was teaching me the Truth. Dwell on these things. Do what you have learned . . . and the God of peace will be with you.

And so I prayed, "Lord, help me to dwell on Your good things. Not on my present circumstances, but on all of the true, honorable, just, pure, lovely, commendable things You have done. Help me to dwell on that."

Then Paul, thanking the church at Philippi for their care and concern for him in chains, went on, ". . . for I have learned to be content in whatever circumstances I am" (v. 11). This was it. I was all ears.

> I know both how to have a little, and I know how to have a lot. In any and all circumstances I have learned the secret of

being content—whether well fed or hungry, whether in abundance or in need. I am able to do all things through Him who strengthens me. Still, you did well by sharing with me in my hardship. (vv. 12–14)

I am able to do all things through Him who strengthens me. Was that the first time I heard Paul say this quotable phrase as he actually meant it? I always thought this line meant I could achieve all things, but this was so much more meaningful. Paul was saying that he could endure and even rejoice in all things—all kinds of circumstances—through Christ who was the source of his strength.

My mind was blown by the Truths the Holy Spirit was teaching me in my grief. Contentment isn't about hanging our hopes on things that truly may never come to pass. Contentment is having hope that is not dependent on our circumstances. It's living with everything we ever wanted or none of the things we really needed, and being joyful either way because we are dwelling on the good things God has already done.

I was learning, maybe for the first time or maybe all over again, that God was good because of who He was, not because of what He could do for me. At the end of a week studying Philippians 4, I was beginning to understand that the secret to being content wasn't unattainable—it was going to take some serious "looking up" from my own circumstances and resting my gaze on the permanent Truth that outlasts them—but I had hope! Hope in a promise that would never pass away. I was fired up, ready to live a content life.

Of course, this lasted for me about as long as manna lasted in the wilderness for the Israelites. I couldn't ride the wave of a week in Philippians 4 all the way to Glory, though I kinda thought it was possible at the time. Contentment was going to be a lifelong exercise in fixing my gaze on the Lord both in plenty and in want. Little did I know the kind of exquisite "want" He had waiting for me, just a couple of weeks later.

HOPE IN GOD

When I was twenty-seven years old, just fourteen months after burying my stillborn daughter, life had become a prolonged study of how unsure and unreliable anything was. Even in the good moments of searching and finding promises of contentment in God's Word, I was more emotionally unstable than ever. Perhaps there's something uniquely hard about that second year of grief, or maybe it was the added heartache of two more losses and a handful of other relational wounds I carried. (It was probably all of the above.)

There were good days and bad days, but the bad days were beginning to come closer together rather than grow further apart. We decided to pursue counseling to help me deal with some of the trauma I was processing.

One Saturday morning I had the French doors in the breakfast nook swung open while I cleaned up the breakfast table. Without any warning, that Katie-girl from one street over tapped her knuckles on the already-open door, just checking in after wrapping up one of her morning walks. She knew life was a little dark and twisty for me, so she faithfully popped in unannounced, just like I needed her to do.

I stood in the doorway with her that morning and started to tremble as I opened my mouth to answer her "how are you this morning?" question. I wasn't well and she could tell. While Katie listened, I listed. I counted all of the things I thought were true over the past year that had become untrue without warning. Beyond babies and births, I talked about family and friends and betrayals and some of the freshest wounds only a few people knew.

"None of these things are true anymore! The only thing I know is that bad things happen. Ryan and Oliver could be gone by the end of the day, and nothing on heaven or earth tells me otherwise!"

She stood still while my body shook as I talked. In my greatest, most honest crisis of faith, Katie faced me and simply agreed. Loving me like the fragile friend I was, she said yes to all of the hard realities I had faced, yes to the possibility of hard realities to come, and she reminded me that I wasn't alone, that real hope never went anywhere. She reminded me that nothing could ever change those two simple facts.

I told her I was all out of hope, and that didn't faze her either. Even better, Katie told me if I could only hope in one thing the rest of my life, I could simply hope in God. I couldn't argue. When the landscape of my life seemed to be in a constant recycle of creation and destruction, He was always there, unchanging, never being created or destroyed.

It wasn't a moment that fixed everything. At the end of Katie's visit I was still very sad, still learning about joy and hope and contentment. But she did put to words the question I'd been needing to ask all along: "Why are you cast down, O my soul?"

Knowing all that I knew, having stored up the Truth of God's Word in my heart, I needed to ask this simple question of myself. This is what the psalmist asks in Psalm 42:5: "Why are you cast down, O my soul, and why are you in turmoil within me?" (ESV). But the psalmist doesn't end there. He gives his own soul a charge—a reminder: "Hope in God; for I shall again praise him, my salvation" (ESV).

"Hope in God."

It was the question. And the answer:
Why are you cast down?
Why the turmoil?
Hope in God.

Katie was right—the psalmist was right. This was the hope I had been looking for—the hope that was sure, that wouldn't betray me or succumb to physical limitations, and would surely rise with the sun the next morning. I knew this because God's Word promised it (Hos. 6:3). When my soul was cast down—and it had been more often than not those days—I was finally content knowing I didn't need to hope in a hundred things. I could simply hope in God. He was more sure than the sun, faithful in my life as He was in the lives of men and women written about in His Word.

Content in my singular, not-passing-away hope, I was learning to breathe in and out and to rejoice in my own version of hardship, just like Paul.

EVERYTHING IS UNDER CONTROL

The very next weekend, Ryan and Oliver left me at home for a Saturday morning of house cleaning. (Cleaning my house is something I truly enjoy, but only when I'm alone!) I started in the master bathroom, which was also our only downstairs bathroom, so it had seen its share of . . . traffic.

Feeling particularly orderly, I took a little extra time to straighten the under-sink cabinets and discovered an unused pregnancy test from a few months earlier. In an effort to exercise my newfound contentment, I decided to throw it away. Healthy pregnancies were off the table for us, and our efforts had been concentrated on preventing future grief. No need for this guy—I was content.

Of course, it seemed wasteful to toss a perfectly good pregnancy test in the trash—like when you tear off one too many paper towels. You can't just throw it away; you have to wipe something with it! So, in order to justify throwing it away, I took a quick *ahem* bathroom break. Capping the test, I left it on the bathroom counter, and moved on to vacuum the upstairs.

More than an hour later, the upstairs was straightened, wiped, vacuumed, and mopped. It felt nice to have control over something in my life, even if it was just dust bunnies and dirty laundry. I headed back to the master bathroom to put a few things in their place, when the completely forgotten test caught my attention out of the corner of my eye. I reached for it to toss it in the garbage, barely glancing at the results as I mentally checked one more item off my list.

As the test fell out of my hands and into the trash can, I saw it: the word "not" was missing from the "not pregnant" display. Confident I was just seeing it from a bad angle, I reached into the trash can, brushing aside tissues and a few cotton balls, and picked it up. Then I just stood there, staring.

PREGNANT.

I hit my knees.

No. Please, no. I can't take this again. My heart is so wounded, Lord, why would You do this? We truly cannot bear another loss!

A few minutes earlier, I was a woman from a Febreze commercial, going about my Saturday cleaning routine. I had things under control. And now I was back in that place of impending grief and no control where I'd found myself so many times before. It was as if a semitruck had just plowed through my front door and slammed me on the floor between the bathroom and the kitchen.

Face in the carpet, tears flowing freely, I prayed to the God who gives and takes away—who sustains every life and gives every breath—that He would let us keep this baby. If God gave this child to us, would He please give us a life with it?

Lord, I will hope in You. I cannot bear to hope for this, but I can hope in You.

I repeated Philippians 4:4–6 to myself, mumbling out loud through tears: "Rejoice in the Lord always. I will say it again: Rejoice! . . . The Lord is near. Don't worry about anything, but in everything, through prayer and petition with thanksgiving, let your requests be made known to God."

The Lord is near. Don't worry, but let your requests be made known.

I prayed the last verse out loud, half claiming it and half begging it to be true: "And the peace of God, which surpasses every thought, will guard your hearts and minds in Christ Jesus."

Lord, guard my heart with Your peace. I don't know how to pick myself up off of this floor without Your promises.

Holding as tightly as my feeble heart could manage to the only permanent thing I still knew to be true, I tucked the test into the waistband of my shorts, walked down the street to Katie's house, and knocked on her door. When she answered, she saw my tears for the second time that week and I produced the stick that was supposed to be just a matter of housekeeping. Words weren't necessary. She opened her screen door to join me on the porch and we sunk into the white rocking chairs, staring through her ferns and across her front yard for a long time.

"Katie, I can't. I'm trying, but I can't. Bad things happen to me, not good things." I knew my hope in God meant He would be with me in joy and sorrow, but this was still so intimidating. So menacing.

"Well, I'm excited," she said with the genuine effervescence that only Katie could pull off in such a dramatic moment. "I think you're going to get to keep this baby!" Katie isn't naive and had only been real and straightforward with me up till now. I really appreciated her hoping for me, but I could only look at her through tired, puffy eyes as I fumbled with the test in my hands. Silence hung in the air.

Then Katie said, "You know you carried something you peed on all the way to my house, right?" An involuntary chuckle escaped before I could stop it.

"I can't hope for this. I have no guarantee. And I'm all out of any other kind of hope."

"I know. We can just hope in God. And for this baby? I'll hope enough for the both of us."

BUT THIS I CALL TO MIND

One of my favorite demonstrations of the relationship between suffering and hope in Scripture is found in the book of Lamentations. Many of us are only familiar with the middle four verses of this book, but the real beauty is that those lines of confident hope are situated symmetrically among an exactly equal number of chapters and verses of some of the deepest lament the Bible contains. The profound sorrow surrounding these chapters is what makes them beautiful:

> He has made my teeth grind on gravel,
> and made me cower in ashes;
> my soul is bereft of peace;
> I have forgotten what happiness is;
> so I say, "My endurance has perished;
> so has my hope from the LORD." (Lam. 3:16–18 ESV)

The lamentor (many people believe Lamentations was written by the prophet Jeremiah, but not everyone agrees) poetically describes his circumstances and even the way he has responded to them in a way that is honest and relatable.

Only a few verses later, it's as if the writer pauses, lifts his eyes from the cup of sorrow he holds in his hands, and looks to the Lord Himself. He writes:

> But this I call to mind,
> and therefore I have hope:
> The steadfast love of the LORD never ceases;
> his mercies never come to an end;
> they are new every morning;
> great is your faithfulness.
> "The LORD is my portion," says my soul,
> "therefore I will hope in him." (Lam. 3:21–24 ESV)

Then, mysteriously yet honestly, his eyes lower once again to the cup of still-warm sorrow and he resumes the book with exactly two and a half more chapters of lamenting. Only this time, his lamenting is laced with hope:

> Let him sit alone in silence
> when it is laid on him;
> let him put his mouth in the dust—
> there may yet be hope. (Lam. 3:28–29 ESV)

This was me. Maybe it has been you, too. Looking down, feeling honest, unignorable sorrow, and lifting my eyes each morning to "call to mind" the steadfast love of the Lord. And every morning, breathing in Truth like air, I would rise with these words on my tongue:

> "The LORD is my portion," says my soul,
> "therefore I will hope in Him." (ESV)

EXCESSIVE EPITAPHS

I won't make you scan ahead to learn that the headline of the next nine months was this: by the grace of a never-stopped-being-faithful God, I had a textbook pregnancy and delivery. Her name is Hazel, a Hebrew name which translates, "look to God."

Now, I want to be clear. God's faithfulness is independent of and unaffected by our present circumstances. I say "never-stopped-being-faithful" because that pregnancy and delivery aren't the things that made God faithful, and we would be missing something foundational to believe they were.

Think about that for a second. If God's faithfulness were dependent on our good days and our bad days, that would mean His faithfulness changes with the wind, even from person to person. That would give credence to statements like this: "I'm having a good day, so my God is faithful, but you're having a tragic year, so your God is less faithful." It's just not true. James 1:17 tells us God "does not change like shifting shadows" (NIV). He is one God, and He has one way.

Having a healthy baby after losing five others does not mean that God was finally good to us or finally on our side. He was faithful through every loss, every ache, every joy. God was permanent when even our own children passed away.

It also feels worth saying out loud that contentment is not a formula which produces the thing you want the moment you finally decide you can live without it. In my case, God was doing work in my heart in the area of contentment while growing a child in my womb I didn't know about. This miracle would not serve to erase my anxiety, but to call me out into a much deeper water of trust in His sovereign plan—a very scary place for me. Finding out I was pregnant was not the fairy-tale bow at the end of my tale of woe. It was a humbling exercise of faith—faith in a God who I knew in my head to be good, but felt in my heart that His goodness might equal me not getting what I wanted.

God was good the day we left the hospital after a delivery with no baby in our arms. And He was good the day we left the hospital with Hazel Wren strapped into her car seat.

Two very different days. The very same God.

I wish I could say I was calm and grateful and 100 percent at peace through my pregnancy with Hazel, thrilled just to be carrying another baby. But, as you can imagine, I was not. I was a mess of every wounded/healing/terrified/excited emotion a mother carrying a baby after a loss can feel—amplified by pregnancy hormones, of course. (I was a real joy. Just ask Ryan.)

There was one particular instance when I was six months along that still makes me cringe with compassion for my post-trauma pregnant self.

I was using the self-checkout at Home Depot by myself one afternoon, and somehow or another, enough static energy had built up between me, the rug, and the machine that when I reached to touch the screen, I received a pretty jarring electrical shock. It didn't harm the baby, but I didn't know that. I drove home in tears, confident the shock had stopped her heart, then spent the next three hours lying still on the sofa, waiting to feel movement. As I cried and waited, I did the only thing that felt natural for me to do: I toiled over an epitaph for a second tiny headstone in Harpeth Hills Cemetery.

"What are we going to write on a *second* headstone?" I sobbed to Ryan.

"Babe, maybe we should just call the midwife?"

Poor Ryan. He put up with a version of this scenario every other week until she was born. He was scared too—terrified, in fact. But we were raising a three-year-old and trying to not lose our minds, so we could really only afford to have one parent at a time planning imaginary memorial services.

HAZEL

Hazel turned out to be the life of the party.

She is six years old now, and everywhere she goes, she brings a spark of joy to go with her ocean-blue eyes and white-blond hair. Our breakfast table feels just right nowadays, complete enough until Jesus makes all thing new.

We were surprised with another pregnancy after Hazel and another too-soon goodbye to that baby, too. God was good and faithful and with us in that season, just like He was in the seasons before. If anything, our own ever-changing journey of joy and sorrow has made plain the unchanging steadfastness of our God. It's as if a time lapse of our lives is the only way to truly see all that is always changing, and the One who was permanent all along.

That is our hope. Not that things will work out for our benefit. Not that our lives will look the way we wanted them to. And not that we would be spared from suffering.

Our hope is in the One who has never failed to fulfill His promises to us. We hope in the One who has only ever been faithful in our own lives, and since the beginning of time. Our hope is in God alone.

SHE READS TRUTH

PSALM 42:5 ESV

Why are you cast down, O my soul,
*   and why are you in turmoil within me?*
Hope in God; for I shall again praise him,
*   my salvation.*

HOSEA 6:1-3 ESV

"Come, let us return to the L*ord*;
*   for he has torn us, that he may heal us;*
*   he has struck us down, and he will bind us up.*
After two days he will revive us;
*   on the third day he will raise us up,*
*   that we may live before him.*
Let us know; let us press on to know the L*ord*;
*   his going out is sure as the dawn;*
he will come to us as the showers,
*   as the spring rains that water the earth."*

HABAKKUK 3:17-19 ESV

Though the fig tree should not blossom,
* nor fruit be on the vines,*
the produce of the olive fail
* and the fields yield no food,*
the flock be cut off from the fold
* and there be no herd in the stalls,*
yet I will rejoice in the LORD;
* I will take joy in the God of my salvation.*
GOD, the Lord, is my strength;
* he makes my feet like the deer's;*
* he makes me tread on my high places.*

ROMANS 5:3-4

And not only that, but we also rejoice in our afflictions, because we know
that affliction produces endurance, endurance produces proven character, and
proven character produces hope.

TAKE A SEAT

God's Sovereignty Is Permanent
When Our Power Is Passing Away

H *uh. He's older than I expected.*
    That's what I remember thinking when the psychologist walked into his office, where I sat waiting, visibly uncomfortable, in an armchair in front of his desk. My hasty observation was quickly followed by a feeling of dread. *There's no way he's going to understand me.*

It took quite a bit of coaxing for me to concede to sitting in that chair, in that office on the other side of town. A dear friend had sat in the same chair months before, and she gently encouraged me to take the step. My husband supported it, too, though I think he wished it hadn't come to this. I felt the same. *Was this the right call? Did I really want to know what I'd come there to find out?* I didn't know. All I knew was something had to give. The cost of ignoring the signs was one I was unwilling to pay.

I offered timid answers to the doctor's questions, explaining how the past two years had unfolded. I told him about the unexpected twin pregnancy and how I stayed home full-time with those beautiful baby boys and their big sister. I told him about Dad, from the heart attacks to the funeral and the long road in-between. I told him about our finances, about the short sale and the foreclosure and our commission-based income that ebbed more than it flowed. And I told him about me, how I'd handled it all—or rather, not handled it all. I told him about the panic attacks and the fear, and about how it felt like I was watching myself live out my days but could not control my own reactions.

I said it all out loud—laid it out like items from a backpack I'd been carrying uphill and couldn't put down. I said all the words I'd been too scared to say to anyone else, and I said it with guilt hanging on my every word. Hearing those stories fill the room that day, I felt equal parts relieved and ashamed.

When I finished, something magical happened. The man I expected to look at me over his glasses, eyes full of disapproval as he told me how to get right all I'd been getting awfully wrong, did something else instead. He nodded his head, looked at me with care and compassion, and said, no hint of irony in his tone, "I'm surprised you made it this far."

Oh! Oh. You mean it's okay that I can't carry it all? It's okay that I'm buckling under the pressure?

I don't remember exactly what I said in response, but I do remember exactly what I felt. I felt seen. I felt relieved. I felt understood in a way I had not even understood myself for months and months on end—and this from a man forty years my senior whom I'd met only an hour earlier.

I felt lighter, like someone had come along and lifted that heavy pack off my shoulders for a minute, just long enough for me to take one deep, slow breath.

Praise the Lord for health professionals.

I'd been trying so hard. I'd done my best to keep myself and my world together. But I couldn't. In tightening my grip, I was crushing the people I loved; I was crushing myself. In resolving to hold it together, I was rapidly falling apart. And the incredible thing was this: the doctor was not surprised. He did not look at me as if I should have been strong enough to shoulder this load alone. He looked at me as if I was never meant to.

I walked out of the office that day still feeling the weight of a hundred worries on my shoulders, and I sat sobbing in the front seat of my parked minivan for a good, long while. But these tears were not tears of panic. They were not tears of hopelessness or fear or even sadness. They were tears of humble relief. Jesus had met me at the end of my rope in the place I least expected Him—in a psychologist's office in a suburb of Nashville, Tennessee—and He had held out the Truth that had never stopped being true.

I am not the holder-together of all things. I was never meant to be.

THE ILLUSION OF CONTROL

God's Word says Christ holds all things together. Not you. Not me. I know. I was shocked, too. But it's there in black and white. Look:

> He is the image of the invisible God,
> the firstborn over all creation.
> For everything was created by Him,
> in heaven and on earth,
> the visible and the invisible,
> whether thrones or dominions
> or rulers or authorities—
> all things have been created through Him and for Him.
> He is before all things,
> and by Him all things hold together. (Col. 1:15–17)

By Him, not Amanda, do all things hold together. Nevertheless, I start out most days wondering how I'm going to do just that—hold all the things together. I wonder how I'll manage to be the glue that my family, my work, my sanity will need to get from daylight to dusk.

It's the main ingredient of the fall (see Genesis 3) as well as its primary effect—our need to control, our desire to create our own truth, to find our own way, to manipulate our circumstances to match our desires. Somewhere in the Garden, the Serpent must have whispered slowly and deliberately into Eve's ear, "It's all up to you, my dear." And we pass the lie down from one generation to the next, like a childhood game of telephone gone dangerously wrong.

Three years before I sat sobbing in the parking lot of the psychologist's office, I sat on the couch in our living room, looking into the tired eyes of my kind, strong, and stressed-out husband. He had just walked in the door from his first night of general contractor school, the first official step of an anticipated and reluctant career change.

The music industry is a tough place to make a living, and David, who managed musicians, was growing weary. He was weary of the fight to keep the business he loved afloat, a business he'd been growing for twenty hard-fought years. He was weary of the way commission and clients come and go with little warning, the frustrating reality that hard work doesn't always pay off the way you hope it will. Music was a roller coaster, and we'd decided it was time for our family of three to unbuckle our seat belts and exit the ride.

Our daughter, not quite two years old at the time, was asleep in the other room. We'd always wanted a large family—large to us, anyway. And that sleeping, spunky girl with a very big personality and very little hair was the best first installment of our dream that we could have imagined. But family life was hard. I'm not sure why it surprised us; we're fairly down-to-earth folks. We loved each other fiercely, but love couldn't pay the mortgages we struggled to keep current, or the medical bills we were still paying from when our bundle of spunk was born. Love was enough and not enough, all at once. And we were nervous.

There we sat on the sofa, my David and me, as he told me about his first night of class. But the conversation wasn't about excitement for what he'd learned about his potential new trade; it was about the price of the books, the length of the class, the doubt that he could do this, too, on top of everything else. We'd been right, he said. This was definitely not the time to think about having Child No. 2. Our dream of raising four kids in the heart of the city would have to wait. It was the responsible—and realistic—thing to do.

I remember watching the words come out of his mouth and knowing he was right. And I remember being unable to find my own words in response; because I was 90 percent sure I was already pregnant.

[Pause—I know we've had a lot of baby talk in this book. Babies are a part of our stories, and we can't—and don't want to—rewrite them. We also know that for you out there, our dear readers and friends, babies are not a part of all of your stories. Your story is your story, and it's different from ours. The characters are different, the timing is different, the setting is different. And that's not just okay—that is by God's loving design! The details of our stories are different, but the God who writes our stories is the same. His gospel and His glory shine through each and every chapter, wherever the plot line takes us. This said, please, if babies ever become part of your story, do not do to your husband what I am about to do to mine. Bless his heart, you guys.—Unpause]

With nothing more than a quiet word of "I'll be right back," I stood up from that sofa where my husband was sitting. I walked upstairs to our bathroom, took a test that confirmed my suspicions, walked back down the stairs, and took my place back on that sofa. I looked at my worried husband through worried eyes, put my hand on his knee, swallowed hard and said, "We're pregnant."

Silence.

We didn't say much more that night. I'm sad to say we didn't even smile. We just stared at each other, terrified. No just-can't-wait phone calls to our parents. No celebratory glasses of fizzy soda. No laughter. Just fear.

A few weeks later, we had our first doctor's visit. We were smiling by then, having discovered that if we couldn't bring ourselves to feel excited about the timing of this baby, we could tell others and let them be excited for us. Eventually, our hearts followed their lead. David had set aside his career change and dug his heels back into the business he loved in spite of itself. I had postponed my plans to finally finish the graduate degree I'd walked away from years before. We were allowing ourselves to joyfully anticipate this little girl- or boy-to-be who would soon make our family a party of four.

We sat in the waiting room, observing the other expectant parents and their children. A woman who was noticeably pregnant with multiples fidgeted uncomfortably in her seat across the room from us, and I patted my already-growing belly and whispered jokingly to David, "At least it's not twins!"

We left our appointment an hour later with a long string of ultrasound pictures, our faces white as ghosts. Two babies. "Looks like they're identical!" the doctor had declared. Two babies. Two.

That autumn our identical boys were born. I quit my full-time job and we pulled our daughter out of day care. And just like that, I went from being a working mom of one to a stay-at-home mom of three under three. It was the hardest thing I'd ever done. The best, but easily the hardest.

The next twelve months is stuck in fast-forward in my memory. I can only see glimpses of the still images here and there—nothing much more than that.

I see my daughter in pajamas, reading board books to the boys, sitting on the floor between their bouncy seats while morning light from our big, bungalow windows streams in. I see David changing diapers in the dark, handing me one boy to nurse and then the other, then lying next to us on the bed, waiting to carry them back to the crib they shared in the tiny alcove of our bedroom.

I see friends standing in the doorway holding casseroles and bags of salad, cups of coffee from our favorite coffee shop, and plastic containers full of cookies. I see my dad holding the babies while my mom colors a picture at the dining room table with my daughter, who is narrating the event with a made-up song.

I see high chairs in the kitchen and two big black dogs sleeping on hardwood floors in the sun, the crabapple tree in full bloom just outside the window.

I can't quite see the anxiety that filled in the cracks of our new life, but I can remember how it felt.

FAILURE

The next fall, just before the babies turned one, my dad had his first heart attack while driving to Nashville to start house hunting with my mom. They'd come up nearly every month since the boys were born to help us navigate these new chaotic waters, and they were ready to make their return to Tennessee official. We were thrilled.

The string of illnesses and hospital visits would continue for more than two years, marked by miracles and setbacks—those intense periods of time where you feel pummeled by the darkest and richest moments life has to offer, all at once. The daily rhythm of life changed for all of us. My brother stayed in Nashville for stretches of days and weeks, and we spent all of our spare time in the hospital, watching over Mom as she watched over Dad. We adjusted, all of us, but our adjustments felt less like intentional actions and more like feeling our way around in a pitch-black room.

When it came to Dad, we controlled the things we could—fluffing and arranging his pillows, combing his hair the way he liked it, and shaving his face when the stubble grew. We asked all the medical questions and insisted on timely answers. We were there to adjust his nasal cannula when the discomfort made him flinch, there to calm him when the confusion and panic set in. We controlled the things we could. But what we could control wasn't much, not compared to all we couldn't.

We couldn't keep him from pain. We couldn't keep him from dying, and so terribly slowly.

Also in the crowded category of things out of our control, our finances were crumbling. The real estate market David and I had funneled our savings into was imploding, only suddenly instead of slowly. That job I'd left when the boys were born—bringing our two-income family of three to a one-income family of five—happened to be in real estate development. So every day for weeks I donned my best "I know real estate" hat and camped out on the phone, arguing through tears with the woman from the bank, trying in vain to convince her to approve our short-sale paperwork. She could hear the kids playing or fussing in the background, which was convenient for masking the sound of my crying but did no favors for my blood pressure.

I kept calling the bank and taking their calls, providing page after page of our life on paper—the babies, the bills, the state assistance for formula and food. I couldn't control our income and I couldn't stop the flood of shame we felt for not being able to feed our kids on our own. *But I can get us through this,* I thought. *I can fight the good fight with the bank and win by securing the loss. I can at least do THIS.*

The thing I remember most from that year was the dread. The dread I felt when I drove to the hospital, not knowing what this visit would hold. The dread I felt when I swiped the debit card at the grocery store, not knowing if the charge would go through.

That feeling in my chest—the way my heart would clench like a fist and squeeze the air from my lungs—was a constant in these years of uncertainty. Anxiety had become so much a part of my insides that I couldn't recognize it for what it was. It was so tangible and thick I would have sworn I could hold it in my hands like a brick, yet I couldn't call it out. I couldn't give it a name. And so I called it what it looked like.

I called it failure.

It was my job to control the things in my reach, to make sure my people were okay at all times. And I was failing. I was failing miserably.

CONFESSIONS

I love David's psalms (of course, I'm referring to David the shepherd-king in the Bible, though my David is fairly poetic in his own right).

I especially love them for their honesty. Honest words are an electric combination of boldness and humility, of openness and resolve—like an injection of fresh air in a locked, windowless room. I've always loved words, but honest words are my favorite.

David's psalms are also true; they're part of God's Word. Honest, true words are a life-giving oxygen all their own.

When I think on those years when anxiety roared like a fire inside my chest, it isn't hard to imagine King David's words as my own. His psalms of petition and lament to God make me feel not just heard, but understood. Listen to the desperation in Psalm 6, titled in my Bible "A Prayer for Mercy":

> LORD, do not rebuke me in Your anger;
> do not discipline me in Your wrath.
> Be gracious to me, LORD, for I am weak;

heal me, LORD, for my bones are shaking;
my whole being is shaken with terror.
And You, LORD—how long?

Turn, LORD! Rescue me;
save me because of Your faithful love.
For there is no remembrance of You in death;
who can thank You in Sheol?

I am weary from my groaning;
with my tears I dampen my pillow
and drench my bed every night.
My eyes are swollen from grief;
they grow old because of all my enemies.

Depart from me, all evildoers,
for the LORD has heard the sound of my weeping.
The LORD has heard my plea for help;
the LORD accepts my prayer.
All my enemies will be ashamed and shake with terror;
they will turn back and suddenly be disgraced.

Can you hear yourself in that psalm? The you of today, or the you of some day in the past? I can. I can hear the me that was desperate for control, aching for relief. *I am weak. My bones are shaking. My whole being is shaken with terror. Rescue me.*

In another of David's psalms—Psalm 55—he dares to say what most of us only think when circumstances are so dire: I'd fly away from here if I could.

Hear his confession of fear from verses 4–8:

My heart shudders within me;
terrors of death sweep over me.

Fear and trembling grip me;
horror has overwhelmed me.
I said, "If only I had wings like a dove!
I would fly away and find rest.
How far away I would flee;
I would stay in the wilderness. *Selah*
I would hurry to my shelter
from the raging wind and the storm."

I've said these words too. *Send me to the wilderness, Lord; anywhere but here. I'm tired, Lord. Won't You give me rest? How long, O Lord?*

I wonder if you, too, have ever felt paralyzed by despair, immovable in your weakness. I wonder if your voice has ever ached from crying so loud and long, asking, *Is God going to show up?* So did David.

This is from Psalm 69:

Save me, God,
for the water has risen to my neck.
I have sunk in deep mud, and there is no footing;
I have come into deep waters,
and a flood sweeps over me.
I am weary from my crying;
my throat is parched.
My eyes fail, looking for my God. (vv. 1–3)

That's why I love the Psalms. So much honesty in so few words. So much real, heart-wrenching, gut-punching pain and fear from a man who truly loved and sought to honor the Lord (Acts 13:22).

These psalms do not record God's answer to David's plea, but that does not mean God is silent.

We do not always feel God's presence or hear the Holy Spirit respond to us when we pray. That, too, does not mean God is silent.

If we broaden our view from David's specific suffering and cry for help, if we zoom out and look around and listen, we can better see and hear God moving. God is unchanging (Heb. 13:8), unchangeable (Mal. 3:6), and He is not bound by time or space or any other created thing (Ps. 102:25–27). So what is true of God now, was true of God while David was crying out from the caves when he feared for his life. What is true of God then, is true of God now as we call out to Him from our hard, hurting places.

God said this to the people of Israel through the prophet Isaiah, to encourage them in their coming exile and deliverance:

> "Remember this and be brave;
> take it to heart, you transgressors!
> Remember what happened long ago,
> for I am God, and there is no other;
> I am God, and no one is like Me.
> I declare the end from the beginning,
> and from long ago what is not yet done,
> saying: My plan will take place,
> and I will do all My will." (Isa. 46:8–10)

Can you believe that? God has declared "from long ago what is not yet done" (v. 10). His plans involve us, but they are not dependent on us. God's sovereignty remains, even when our power is slipping away.

It's true, but when we're up to our necks like David, it's hard to believe.

Jesus offered a gentle but unwavering reminder of the Father's power to those gathered to hear His teaching now known as the Sermon on the Mount. The verses are normally used to encourage us not to worry about material things because God will provide us what we need. And that's true. But there's more to it than that. See if you think so, too.

> "Look at the birds of the air: they neither sow nor reap nor gather into barns, and yet your heavenly Father feeds them.

Are you not of more value than they? And which of you by being anxious can add a single hour to his span of life? And why are you anxious about clothing? Consider the lilies of the field, how they grow: they neither toil nor spin, yet I tell you, even Solomon in all his glory was not arrayed like one of these. But if God so clothes the grass of the field, which today is alive and tomorrow is thrown into the oven, will he not much more clothe you, O you of little faith?" (Matt. 6:26–30 ESV)

God's care for the birds and the lilies is not dependent on the birds and the lilies.

There is a lake around the corner from my house. Some mornings on my way to work, I pull my car into the parking lot near the boat ramps and walk down the bank, through the picnic tables and trees to the shoreline. I take my seat on a large piece of driftwood and sit quietly for a while, watching the water wash rhythmically over the rocks and the geese bounce softly on the glassy surface. I observe the color of the sky and the formation of the clouds, and listen to the wind shake the leaves. There's a tree-covered island in the middle of the lake, and occasionally something will startle the birds and send them flying in and out of the tall green mass, squawking and diving and chasing each other in circles.

I go there to remember that God is God and I am not.

From my spot beside the lake I can see a whole world that exists without any help from me. The water, the wind, the birds, the sky—it's all there, every day, every time I take time to stop and look. It's a whole world that carries on apart from me, yet it is only a tiny sliver of the world our God upholds by His power and His Word.

I go to the lake to remember that I don't have to grasp for control because the control is already His. And He is good.

The David of the Bible knew this. Even when he couldn't see God's hand, he trusted God was there—not just passively watching, but actively exercising His sovereignty as He always has (Exod. 7:1–5).

David could look back and remember the times that God delivered His people. I can look back and remember the times that He delivered and cared for me, even when I wasn't aware of it and didn't do one tiny little thing to help. And if I'm having trouble remembering, I can go to the lake and glimpse a whole world that He sustains without my help. Shocking, but true.

The other day I almost drove by without stopping, saying hurriedly to the Lord, "I don't have time today to stop and pray."

I could sense His Spirit's response: *All of time is Mine. You'll have what I give you.*

FREE TO REST

That first day at the psychologist's office, he described anxiety as an internal security guard. "Everyone has one," he said. "A certain level of anxiety is necessary." The security guard in us helps us know when to act and when to worry; it's what gives us a healthy level of caution, he said.

He also said that most people's internal security guard does its regular rounds, then sits down until the next round. But not mine. Mine was casing the place constantly, never stopping, never resting.

I knew in an instant he was right. My security guard was on high alert, all the time. I was pacing around to protect all the things. I was fighting to hold everyone and everything together. I thought all the battles were mine to fight, and I thought I was losing them all. It was just a silly analogy, but it helped me understand.

I told the doctor about the day before I called his office to make the appointment. My daughter was five years old at the time and still so little.

Her brothers were two. They were (and still are) all-heart and all-energy, impossible to tame and impossible not to love.

She was taking a bath and one of the boys walked up to the side of the old clawfoot tub to jabber and hit things and play. She didn't want them there, a reasonable feeling for a five-year-old, so she splashed him and pushed his chubby hands off the side of the tub. He slipped on the bathroom tile and hit his head on the vanity, wailing loudly on contact. I scooped him up in a hurry and examined him. He was fine. I was not.

It was my job to keep our children safe. My job to keep our bills paid. My job to keep my dad alive. My job to hold all things together. I couldn't do those things, and I panicked.

I yelled at my daughter, carted the boys to the safety of the other room, and came back to yell some more. She cried and cried, knowing she'd done something wrong, but not understanding why Mama was reacting the way I was. Truth was, I didn't understand it either. She was confused, and I was scared. I was terrified.

The brick in my chest caught fire that day. I left the room, leaned against the kitchen cabinets, and gripped the counter so hard it hurt my hands. I cried loud, hot tears and forced myself to take ragged breaths in and out, in and out. I found a mirror and in it found a person I didn't fully recognize, a person spinning out of control in ways that made her sad and tired, ashamed and afraid. I was so afraid.

That was the day I decided to make the appointment. I'd been gripping as hard as I could to a control that was not real, and that was the day I knew it was time to unclench my bloodied fists.

I needed my security guard to sit down; I just didn't know it.

We didn't talk about God that day, but His Word is the only thing that brings real hope to this equation. The reality is, even a perfectly-paced internal security guard cannot give me peace. My powerlessness is real—I cannot control the actions of my children or the health of my loved ones. And no, I certainly cannot add a single hour to my own life.

My power is always passing away, never permanent. But God's sovereignty is forever, unwavering.

The stunning Truth of the gospel is that the very power and peace of God lives in us through Jesus Christ. It is "the immeasurable greatness of His power to us who believe" (Eph. 1:19).

God's power, demonstrated in Jesus, reaches every corner of creation. He is "the One who fills all things in every way" (Eph. 1:23). Even my darkest days are not outside His dominion.

Oh, the darkness is still there. We feel it press in around us through our circumstances and our uncertainties, through death and sin. We even feel it from within us, our sin nature fighting for control and dominion where it has not been given to us. But Truth is still true in the dark. God's Truth does not change when I cannot see it.

In another of David's psalms, he affirms the omnipresence and omnipotence of God by asking this question:

> Where can I go to escape Your Spirit?
> Where can I flee from Your presence?
> If I go up to heaven, You are there;
> if I make my bed in Sheol, You are there.
> If I live at the eastern horizon
> or settle at the western limits,
> even there Your hand will lead me;
> Your right hand will hold on to me.
> If I say, "Surely the darkness will hide me,
> and the light around me will be night"—
> even the darkness is not dark to You.
> The night shines like the day;
> darkness and light are alike to You. (Ps. 139:7–12)

Darkness is not dark to God. You and I don't have to scramble to grab hold of control wherever we can find it. We can read Truth and remember that it's already His. The control is always His. The power is always His. Our security guards can sit and rest awhile, knowing the Creator cares constantly for His creation.

There is a sweet psalm that embodies this promise, and while it isn't written by my husband's namesake, I'd like for you read it. Take note of the promises as you read.

> I lift my eyes toward the mountains.
> Where will my help come from?
> My help comes from the LORD,
> the Maker of heaven and earth.
>
> He will not allow your foot to slip;
> your Protector will not slumber.
> Indeed, the Protector of Israel
> does not slumber or sleep.
>
> The LORD protects you;
> the LORD is a shelter right by your side.
> The sun will not strike you by day
> or the moon by night.
>
> The LORD will protect you from all harm;
> He will protect your life.
> The LORD will protect your coming and going
> both now and forever. (Ps. 121)

When we had two newborn babies at the same time, I wanted so badly to keep them safe. But I could not watch over them every minute. It was impossible. I had to sleep.

Isn't it sweet that the Lord gives us sleep? Some of us have better success sleeping than others, but even so, sleep is required. It is not optional. At some point in our days and weeks, you and I have to stop.

We have to unclench our fists and trust the Lord to watch over us. He never sleeps. His eyes are always on us, even in the dark.

At first read, the promises portrayed in this psalm are all I ever wanted for myself, for my family, for all the things I tried so desperately to protect. "The LORD will protect you from all harm; He will protect your life," verse 7 says. But when we limit this promise to our tangible, earthly lives, we miss its fullness. Our all-powerful God can keep us from physical harm, yes. But what He offers us in the pages of Scripture is so much better than that. He offers us eternal life. Eternal hope. An eternal home in heaven with Him.

Rest in that Truth with me awhile. Let down your guard, and let the sovereign God who created and sustains you hold you close by the Truth of His Word.

EPHESIANS 1:16-23

I never stop giving thanks for you as I remember you in my prayers. I pray that the God of our Lord Jesus Christ, the glorious Father, would give you a spirit of wisdom and revelation in the knowledge of Him. I pray that the perception of your mind may be enlightened so you may know what is the hope of His calling, what are the glorious riches of His inheritance among the saints, and what is the immeasurable greatness of His power to us who believe, according to the working of His vast strength.

He demonstrated this power in the Messiah by raising Him from the dead and seating Him at His right hand in the heavens—far above every ruler and authority, power and dominion, and every title given, not only in this age but also in the one to come. And He put everything under His feet and appointed Him as head over everything for the church, which is His body, the fullness of the One who fills all things in every way.

2 CORINTHIANS 12:7–10 ESV

So to keep me from becoming conceited because of the surpassing greatness of the revelations, a thorn was given me in the flesh, a messenger of Satan to harass me, to keep me from becoming conceited. Three times I pleaded with the Lord about this, that it should leave me. But he said to me, "My grace is sufficient for you, for my power is made perfect in weakness." Therefore I will boast all the more gladly of my weaknesses, so that the power of Christ may rest upon me. For the sake of Christ, then, I am content with weaknesses, insults, hardships, persecutions, and calamities. For when I am weak, then I am strong.

TRUTH IN THE DARK

The Gospel Is Permanent
When Our Belief Is Passing Away

Somewhere in my photo archives lives a certain stash of pictures taken over the course of twenty years, all with one rather peculiar—and, for me, joy-inducing—subject: church signs. I love them so much, I can't even tell you.

In fact, I've been delightedly obsessed with this part of Christian culture for over half my life now, always craning my neck to read the marquees as I drive by, and snapping photos with my phone from nearby red lights and stop signs. I even have a few "favorites" around town— those rare types which consistently walk the tightrope of offering mean- ingful yet non-cheesy sayings to passersby (and, let's be honest, those that do the opposite). Southern-born-and-bred gal that I am, outspoken church signs have been a common sight in my life, and I've never had a problem pulling over the car on a road trip to immortalize the best and the worst of them. (Exhibit A: "Forbidden fruit creates many jams.")

I'm a person who hesitates to broadcast my opinions. Ask me to declare something as simple as my five favorite movies, and I'll hem and haw and eventually change the subject. I think that's why I'm so smitten with church signs. For a certain period of time, the church is summarizing their voice in a singular statement, placing it on the marquee for the whole world to see. Anything beyond a scheduling announcement is a pretty bold move, in my opinion.

As folks who grasp for guarantees at every turn, we like a claim we can stand on—a straightforward declaration of "This is the way it is, period" to display in block letters on our personal-belief marquee. But unless it comes straight from God's Word, every statement we make is just an educated guess. The claims we make, no matter how sure or clever, are only temporary "paper promises" compared to the certainty of God and His covenant. So when I see a church proclaim something like "God answers knee-mail" from their lawn, I am both delighted and perplexed.

I've been thinking about what I would put on my marquee. I know the textbook answers of what Christianity is and Who it is about, but are those the truths my life speaks most clearly?

I've long struggled with a DIY view of faith. I saddled myself with expectations to "do" faith well, to control and manipulate it the way I thought I should be able to control my circumstances. But Scripture says faith is a gift (Eph. 2:8). So why do I spend so much time trying to talk myself out of receiving it?

If we could peek into every heart of every believer since the early Church, I wonder if we'd find that each one of them felt the same. Even the earliest believers tried to make salvation about more than grace through faith (Acts 15:1). Those early disciples believed the gospel of Jesus—and I, too, believe—but our human hearts are fickle and the strength of our conviction wanes. Our muddied-up view will not become crystal clear until we're face-to-face with Jesus in Glory (1 Cor. 13:12).

So, what is our motto? What should we—the striving, doubting, catchphrase-making, waxing and waning Church—put on our marquee?

BELIEF AND UNBELIEF

One of my favorite Bible stories takes place in Mark chapter 9. Jesus had just come down from the Mount of Transfiguration with Peter, James, and John, when they found the rest of the disciples in a heated debate with some religious leaders over a young, demon-possessed boy. Here was Jesus, having just been physically glorified while standing atop a mountain—with none other than Elijah and Moses at His side as the audible voice of God the Father said from a cloud, "This is My beloved Son; listen to Him!" (v. 7)—all in plain view of three of His disciples. Then He comes down from that very mountain to see the rest of His disciples calling into question His power and authority.

"You unbelieving generation!" Jesus said to the crowd, His disciples included (v. 19).

That's how I feel about myself sometimes. I know full well that Jesus is who He says He is; I know He is the Son of God. And still, I call into question His power. His authority. His goodness. *You unbelieving generation*, I say to the mirror, shaking my head in shame.

But Jesus doesn't shake His head in disgust and walk away. Jesus continues the conversation.

"Bring him to Me," Jesus said to them. He asked the boy's father, "How long has this been happening to him?"

"From childhood," the father said. ". . . But if You can do anything, have compassion on us and help us."

This, of course, was an absurd thing to say to the Son of God. "If You can'?" Jesus said to the man. "Everything is possible to the one who believes."

Immediately, Scripture says, the boy's father cried out, "I do believe! Help my unbelief." Then Jesus rebuked the spirit and it came out of the boy, and, taking the hand of the very Son of God, the boy stood up, healed (vv. 19–24).

Immediately. As soon as the father's hopes in Jesus' divinity were reaffirmed, he spoke up—immediately. "I do believe! Help my unbelief."

I'm not one for big, bold statements, but this is one I'll dare to make: Were each and every believer to be transparent with ourselves, with each other, and with our God, we'd admit this man's cry is ours too. We believe! And, oh, how we need His help for our unbelief.

Like that boy's daddy—riddled with doubt and panic, his son convulsing on the ground between him and the One the people called the Son of God—we've no reason to hesitate. Our desperation for Jesus isn't a confession we have to hide; the faith was never our doing to begin with.

We believe! Help our unbelief.

This is the Church's motto. This is the headline on our marquee.

WINNING

The good news of the gospel is that our internal paradox of faith and faithlessness does not disqualify or dismiss us from the saving grace of Jesus Christ.

Think about that for a minute. Stunning, right?

We believe, and we do not believe. We receive the gift of faith, and we try to muster it up on our own. Through the lens of God's Word, we have seen Jesus stand before us, clothed in beauty and radiating God's own glory, yet we question His power. Our belief blows about like a leaf in the wind, but the gospel remains.

We cannot make the Good News any less good, even when our faith is weak.

When I was young and my faith took the form of Vacation Bible School and youth camp, we were taught a boisterous enthusiasm for God and religion, and that wasn't a bad thing. Gatherings of loud music and Jesus cheers, fill-in-the-blank workbooks and campy videos, helped me understand that the Good News was indeed good. It was something to celebrate, something I could be proud of. In a life phase marked by braces and perms and school yard cliques, faith was a fact I did not have to hide. It could be the banner I waved higher than sports or school, boys or best friends. And, for the most part, I did. I'm grateful to the teachers and leaders who first taught me what it means to be "not ashamed of the gospel" (Rom. 1:16).

Naturally, that wasn't all I learned. With the positive, seen effects of this blessed indoctrination came the residual, unseen ones. Over time, there seeped into my heart a belief that faith was "mine," in every sense of the word. Produced by me, of me, in me, for me.

Sitting in the stands of concerts, conferences, or the gym at our Christian school, we yelled gleeful, ear-blistering challenges of "We love Jesus, how 'bout YOU?" to the other side. Who could love Jesus the most? Certainly we could. Certainly I could. Even now, all grown up, I can make faith a competition. I compete with others by way of unspoken comparisons of their life to mine; I compete with myself, setting rules and standards I'm determined not to break; I compete with expectations, both the ones that come from within and without.

Remaining pure, maintaining control, exemplifying faithfulness—these were just a few of my expectations. Being sinful, weak, and broken—this was my reality. I thought the goal of faith was to get from A to B, from sinful to pure, from weak to in control, from broken to fixed. But what if that's not it? What if faith is not a matter of making my faults and failures untrue, but hiding myself in the One who is Himself already and always true?

What if "winning" at faith doesn't mean what I've made it out to mean?

BEGGARS AT THE BEAUTIFUL GATE

Faith is a gift. Not a gift we give ourselves or a reward we somehow earn, but an actual grace—by definition, undeserved. We know this because Scripture tells us so.

Perhaps the most familiar evidence of this is a passage from the book of Ephesians:

> *But God,* who is rich in mercy, because of His great love that He had for us, *made us alive* with the Messiah *even though we were dead* in trespasses. You are saved by grace! . . . For you are saved by grace through faith, and *this is not from yourselves; it is God's gift*—not from works, so that no one can boast. (Eph. 2:4–5, 8–9, emphasis mine)

We were dead. God made us alive. This salvation "by grace through faith" is His gift to us. Seems clear enough, huh?

This passage in Paul's letter to the Philippians is another:

> Just one thing: Live your life in a manner worthy of the gospel of Christ. Then, whether I come and see you or am absent, I will hear about you that you are standing firm in one spirit, with one mind, *working side by side for the faith that comes from the gospel,* not being frightened in any way by your opponents. This is a sign of destruction for them, but of your deliverance—and this is from God. *For it has been given to you on*

Christ's behalf not only to believe in Him, but also to suffer for Him, having the same struggle that you saw I had and now hear that I have. (Phil. 1:27–30, emphasis mine)

Here, Paul instructed the people of the church at Philippi to work together "for the faith" (v. 27), while at the same time contending that faith is a gift from Christ (v. 29). These are not mutually exclusive assertions; faith is a gift, and we are to work for it, or on its behalf. But nowhere does God's Word tell us that faith is a result of the working. Instead, Ephesians 2:9 states the opposite: ". . . not from works, so that no one can boast" (along with Rom. 11:6; Gal. 2:16; and Titus 3:5).

As for me, there must be some glitch hardwired into my brain. Even amid all the evidence to the contrary, I am still quick to see the connection between works and faith as causative (works acting as the cause or producer of faith) rather than symptomatic (works acting as a sign of faith).

It's helpful for me to think of this distinction with James 2:26 in mind: "For just as the body without the spirit is dead, so also faith without works is dead." The Bible is not teaching that works give life to faith, but the other way around. A faith that is living will produce works just as a body that is living will produce breath. If a body is not breathing, it is not alive. If a faith is not working, it isn't alive either.

In Acts 3, when the Church was in its infant stages, Jesus had been executed, risen from the dead, and ascended into heaven in front of His disciples. His followers were growing in number, and they were learning what it meant to be the "body" of believers He had proclaimed them to be. The Holy Spirit had descended upon them, Peter had preached repentance and the forgiveness of sins, and word spread rapidly as their numbers grew.

Peter and John were coming to the temple to pray, when a man who regularly begged at the gate asked them for help. The man had been lame from birth, and Peter healed him in the name of Jesus, right then and there. The man, of course, was crazy with joy, running and leaping and praising the Lord. The temple gate where the miracle occurred had a name; it was called Beautiful (vv. 1–10).

The people who saw the crazy-happy man jumping around on two good legs recognized him as the beggar from the Beautiful Gate, and they were amazed. Listen what Peter said to them:

> Men of Israel, why are you amazed at this? Or why do you stare
> at us, as though we had made him walk by our own power or
> godliness? . . . You killed the source of life, whom God raised
> from the dead; we are witnesses of this. By faith in His name,
> His name has made this man strong, whom you see and know.
> So *the faith that comes through Him* has given him this perfect
> health in front of all of you. (Acts 3:12, 15–16, emphasis mine)

The faith that comes through Jesus made the lame man well. The man was not the origin of his own faith; Jesus was.

Friends, we are that man. We are beggars sitting outside the gate called Beautiful, begging for mercy and pleading for life. We are the ones who leap for joy at the healing given to us by the power and grace of Jesus Christ. Like the apostle Paul when he was still Saul, we are incapable of seeing the beauty of Christ without His causing the scales to fall from our eyes (Acts 9:18). The faith is His and He gives it to us. And we say with that same apostle Paul, "Thanks be to God for His indescribable gift" (2 Cor. 9:15).

But then the crazy joy fades into the business of everyday life, or the worst of circumstances crashes down on our celebration. And we stand, disoriented, trying in vain to fashion our own faith when the gift of the gospel has already been offered us in the perfection of Jesus.

The words of our marquee echo: We believe! Help our unbelief.

And He does. By way of His Word, His work, and even His flawed but favored Church, God gives us the gift of faith not just once, but over and over again. We are forgetful doubters and DIYers, after all. We require His grace just to get through the day, whether we know it or not.

FLOODED

In that phase of life when everything was breaking down, when we were completely overwhelmed, I learned an important life lesson: say yes to help.

When a neighbor asks if they can bring over dinner, say yes. When a friend offers to take your child to the park, say yes. When another one offers to scrub your toilets, say yes, even though the thought of someone seeing the underbelly of the dirtiest room in the house makes you cringe. When you're drowning and someone throws you a life preserver, no matter the color or shape, say yes.

I'd just begun to learn this valuable and useful lesson when our basement flooded. It was May 2010. Our boys were six months old. All of Nashville was under water, and we collectively held our breath as the rivers rose.

By now, you know enough of my story to know how I felt about the matter. I was eternally optimistic on the outside, smiling and telling our daughter everything would be alright. On the inside, I was all knotted up, my anxiety rising with the knee-deep water.

We lived in a colorful, close-knit neighborhood on the edge of downtown, and word spread quickly about which homes were hit the hardest and which ones were in the clear. Those who owned a water pump, or had been lucky enough to rent one before the local home improvement store ran out, emptied their own basements and garages as best they could, then offered them up for the next neighbor.

By the time a kind soul arrived at our door with one of the coveted machines, the water was waist-high in some areas. We tried to get the most important belongings to higher ground, even sending some outside to sit in the rain in a "lesser of two evils" decision. But our people were safe. Several feet and a steep set of stairs stood between the floodwaters and the things that mattered most.

Some of you have experienced devastating flooding—lost your home to nature's vast power. This was certainly not that. We were fine. Our lives were never in danger, only our stuff. Still, it was enough to threaten the fabric of my already threadbare emotional well-being.

Here's why I tell you this story: I want you to picture me, a tired, trying mom of three under three, changing the diapers on three bottoms, nursing two babies while settling Sister in with a snack, reading books and picking up toys, and just generally trying to keep the ship afloat (pun intended) while my husband takes on the futile chore of bailing water out of our basement by the bucketful. Then, I want you to picture this: members of our church family making our problem their own.

I hollered a frantic, "Help!" to our neighbor Duane when the basement refrigerator started floating away, and he was there in record time, wading in and holding the rogue appliance in place while David made a platform for it to stand on. After that mini-emergency came another, and another, until he'd been there all day. Helping. Carrying a burden that wasn't his. Being neighborly and keeping us laughing in the process. (You find some funny and incriminating things when your basement floods. A Debbie Gibson cassette tape and *Top Gun* movie poster, anyone?)

Duane wasn't the only one. Other members of our church's small group came and went throughout the day. They held our babies. They entertained the toddler. They pumped untold gallons of floodwater out of our house, rescued everything from stray flip-flops to boxes of cereal as they floated by, and fished childhood keepsakes out of a waterlogged wooden chest I'd had since I was a girl.

They didn't show up because we'd somehow earned the favor. We needed hands, and they came to lend them. They showed up to show us the gospel in action, to be Truth with feet. Ignoring opportunities for judgment and expectation, they flooded us with grace and genuine, get-your-hands-dirty help. And help is what we all need, for more reasons than muddy water.

HOLD ME UP

The body of Christ, His Church, is one of the most tangible evidences here on this temporary earth of the permanence of the gospel.

She gathers her people for worship and prayer, for confession and edification. She invites them to the table to remember the sacrificial death of Jesus, to give thanks for the indwelling of the Holy Spirit. Throughout space and time, from the first disciples to now, the Church has stood like a neon arrow pointing to the gospel by which it exists. We are the marquee, too, in a way.

We don't just see the arrow on Sundays when we stand and sing the call to worship or sit and listen to the sermon. We see it in the Church's people who sit with us for hours in the waiting room, who ask "How are you?" then hold your gaze until you answer, who rush over to bail water out of a flooding basement. The purpose of the arrow is not to solve your problems, but to remind you of what is true. The Church holds the gospel up high for us to see.

When the Israelites were wandering in the desert, they were attacked by the Amalekites. This was after the Lord delivered them from slavery in Egypt, after He parted the Red Sea so they could cross, after He rained down bread from heaven to satisfy their hunger and caused water to pour from a rock to satisfy their thirst. Just as He rescued and sustained them so many times before, God would do the same during this battle. And

He would choose to do so through a familiar image: Moses' arms raised in the air.

We see this image as Moses stood by the Red Sea, staff in hand, when God divided the sea into two walls (Exod. 14:21), and we see it when Moses raised his arms to strike the rock with his staff, producing water for the people at Horeb (Exod. 17:5–6). And as Joshua led the people into battle against Amalek, Moses' upraised arms determined the outcome of the fight. As long as Moses held up his arms, the Israelites prevailed; when he lowered them, the Amalekites prevailed. So Moses held up his arms.

Then something wonderfully ordinary happened. Moses' arms got tired. Moses, the man God had chosen to deliver His people from bondage and lead them to the Promised Land, needed help.

> When Moses' hands grew heavy, they took a stone and put it under him, and he sat down on it. Then Aaron and Hur supported his hands, one on one side and one on the other so that his hands remained steady until the sun went down. So Joshua defeated Amalek and his army with the sword. (Exod. 17:12–13)

Israel needed Moses to hold up his hands so they could win the battle. And Moses needed Aaron and Hur to help him hold up his hands.

We all need holding up. We all need our arms or our faith propped up by the arms or faith of another. When others live in the gospel and live it out, it helps us do the same. Like Moses and Aaron and Hur, we are all part of the great "cloud of witnesses" and it is our responsibility to point our brothers' and sisters' eyes to Jesus, "the source and perfecter of our faith" (Heb. 12:1–2).

We don't just need help when water is rising, or the sickness is prolonged, or the grief is fresh—we need help all the time. Our forgetfulness came with the fall, but the privilege of reminding one another of the gospel is ours until all that is temporary passes away.

THE FABRIC OF FAITH

In 2013, when She Reads Truth turned one year old, we asked the women of the community to share what the past year of "Women in the Word of God every day" had meant to them. And they did. Video after video came in, featuring the faces of real women telling their real stories about how the Lord had used this accidental ministry to draw them closer to Him.

It was only accidental as far as we humans were concerned, of course. God sovereignly wrote She Reads Truth into the story of His kingdom long before any of us even knew the Internet was a thing. He wrote it into my story, too.

The blessing of She Reads Truth in my life was a classic case of God giving me more than I asked for so that I would see what I really needed—Him.

I sat on my bed on the morning of that one-year anniversary, watching women talk about the effect of God's living and active Word in their lives, and I wept. I wept because they were beautiful, these women, and because listening to their stories felt like meeting a long-lost sister—we'd never met, but we felt connected all the same. I wept because I could feel the pinprick of the Holy Spirit, knitting my heart to the heart of this ministry in a way I'd never experienced with anything outside my own family. I wept because the gospel was true, across lives and countries and continents—nothing we said or didn't say could change that.

I longed for a foolproof recipe of how to do faith well, and God placed me in a world where no recipe would do. He made it my job to know Him, not just know about Him. Behind the scenes of this ministry He was growing, the only viable option was to chase after Him with all my might, holding out His Word to women as I ran. Then wake up the next day and do it again. It became my job to trust. It became my job to believe. It became my job—and it still is—to marvel at the depth and breadth of

His goodness, to see up close the way He has provided, and to praise Him as He continues to provide. There are no words for how grateful I am.

God knows His children and He knows what they need. And—in His sovereign care and His sovereign timing—He gives it to them. He writes faith into our stories, not by any merit or action of our own, but simply because it pleases Him to do so.

In his letters to young churches, the apostle Paul often prayed that these believers who were new to the faith would be carried along by the work of the Holy Spirit within them, not by their own merit. Read this prayer in his first letter to the church at Corinth, and notice on whom the giving and growing of faith rests:

> I always thank my God for you because of *God's grace given to you in Christ Jesus*, that *by Him* you were enriched in everything—in all speech and all knowledge. In this way, the testimony about Christ was confirmed among you, so that you do not lack any spiritual gift as you eagerly wait for the revelation of our Lord Jesus Christ. *He will also strengthen you to the end,* so that you will be blameless in the day of our Lord Jesus Christ. *God is faithful;* you were called *by Him* into fellowship with His Son, Jesus Christ our Lord. (1 Cor. 1:4–9, emphasis mine)

Hear the confidence in this verse from the opening prayer in Paul's letter to the Philippians: "I am sure of this, that He who started a good work in you will carry it on to completion until the day of Christ Jesus" (Phil. 1:6).

We don't have to fret if our feelings of faith seem weaker today than they did yesterday, or worry what will happen when our circumstances challenge our beliefs tomorrow in ways we can't anticipate today. God has written the whole of our stories, start to finish, and what He has written into them—including the faith He gives us through Christ—no one can erase.

When you are in Christ, dear friend, faith is woven into the fabric of your story. Not even death can unravel it.

OXYGEN

There was a time not long ago, a season I've described in these pages, when anxiety and false expectations covered me like a weighted blanket. As if the oxygen had been sucked out of every room, I couldn't catch my breath. Then, slowly, the blanket began to lift. Inch by inch it lifted and the air rushed in—when my family loved me anyway, when the doctor understood, when the church held us up, when the long winter finally gave way to spring—until one day I could breathe again. Not the shallow gasps I'd become used to, but deep, lungs-full, eyes-clear breaths. It felt like coming back to life.

That heavy quilt of circumstance was real and it was stifling, but the gospel was always true, even when the heaviness covered me.

The gospel is not only for the moment Christ calls us to repent and follow Him. It is for every moment before and every moment after.

It is for our times of joy and fervor, and our times of doubt and despair.

It is for the day we stand basking in the bright light of hope, and the day we hide, head in hands, in the dark corners of our fear.

It is for the hour that just passed and the hour to come, the situation we just stepped out of and the one we're walking into.

We need it every minute. The gospel is our oxygen.

But, here in our temporary home, the gospel can seem intangible and hard to hang on to. So where do we turn when the heavy blanket is closing in, when we're in the dark, gasping for air?

We turn to God's Word.

When we turn its pages and take in its Truth, the very breath of God fills our lungs, our heart, our mind, our soul. Whether we come to Him doubting, praising, weeping, laughing, His Word is for us and it is true. In this ever-fading world, God's Word never fades. We can approach it in any condition, under any circumstance, and IT IS STILL TRUE.

When our will is weak, God's Word is true.

When our faith is fragile, God's Word is true.

When our hearts are heavy, God's Word is true.

When we wonder if we even believe it, God's Word is true.

The gospel is permanent, even when our belief buckles under the world's weight.

The gospel is the reason we can take Paul seriously when he writes, "Rejoice always! Pray constantly. Give thanks in everything" (1 Thess. 5:16–18). It is the reason we can put away our faith formulas and walk side by side with the One who wrote faith into our stories and has promised to finish what He started. It is the reason a girl who's made promises to God and broken them all can wake up each new day and invite hundreds of thousands of women to read Truth—the Truth about the promise God has made to them, and even to her, and how He has kept and still keeps it, every day.

I am basking in the bright light of hope today, but that weighted blanket may be waiting in the wings. Maybe you're under it now. Jesus promised His disciples they'd have trouble, and we're guaranteed to have it too (John 16:33; 1 Pet. 4:12).

Darkness and death are weighty, and our emotions, our actions, even our beliefs may bend at their pressure. But our God does not. Even under the blanket, we can echo the prayer of Hannah:

> There is no one holy like the LORD.
> There is no one besides You!
> And there is no rock like our God. (1 Sam. 2:2)

Let your chest rise and fall today with the knowledge that the gospel is true. It is oxygen, available every moment of every day, and you can breathe it in.

SHE READS TRUTH

ACTS 2:38-39; 3:1-16

"Repent," Peter said to them, "and be baptized, each of you, in the name of Jesus Christ for the forgiveness of your sins, and you will receive the gift of the Holy Spirit. For the promise is for you and for your children, and for all who are far off, as many as the Lord our God will call."

Now Peter and John were going up together to the temple complex at the hour of prayer at three in the afternoon. And a man who was lame from birth was carried there and placed every day at the temple gate called Beautiful, so he could beg from those entering the temple complex. When he saw Peter and John about to enter the temple complex, he asked for help. Peter, along with John, looked at him intently and said, "Look at us." So he turned to them, expecting to get something from them. But Peter said, "I don't have silver or gold, but what I have, I give you: In the name of Jesus Christ the Nazarene, get up and walk!" Then, taking him by the right hand he raised him up, and at once his feet and ankles became strong. So he jumped up, stood, and started to walk, and he entered the temple complex with them—walking, leaping, and praising God. All the people saw him walking and praising God, and they recognized that he was the one who used to sit and beg at the Beautiful Gate of the temple complex. So they were filled with awe and astonishment at what had happened to him.

While he was holding on to Peter and John, all the people, greatly amazed, ran toward them in what is called Solomon's Colonnade. When Peter saw this, he addressed the people: "Men of Israel, why are you amazed at this? Or why do you stare at us, as though we had made him walk by our own power or godliness? The God of Abraham, Isaac, and Jacob, the God of our fathers, has glorified His Servant Jesus, whom you handed over and denied in the presence of Pilate, when he had decided to release Him. But you denied the Holy and Righteous One and asked to have a murderer given to you. You killed the source of life, whom God raised from the dead; we are witnesses of this. By faith in His name, His name has made this man strong, whom you see and know. So the faith that comes through Him has given him this perfect health in front of all of you."

DECAYING TREASURES

Making the Permanent Thing Our Ultimate Thing

There is a stone chapel on the corner of Church and 3rd in our tiny downtown in Franklin, Tennessee. Our family has attended this church for nearly a decade, and our personal history there is significant.

This is the place where we stood before the church and claimed God's covenant promises for our children. It's where the body of Christ became real to us for the first time as we joined together to meet needs, connect generations, and develop rhythms as a new church plant. It's where we memorized Scripture as a congregation, and where we cobbled together our very first church directory by taking photos under the cherry blossom tree out front, printing copies at a local print shop.

We stood outside this building one Sunday afternoon when a boy climbed too high in one of the trees. A branch broke and he landed hard on the ground right next to us. He wasn't hurt, so maybe that's why it's okay that we still laugh about the boy falling from the sky and his dad scolding him for tree climbing in his church clothes.

As our church plant grew beyond fire-marshal-approved capacity—kids sitting in window wells, dads lining the walls—we prayed and sent yet another group out to plant a new church to preach and live the gospel in another part of town.

In the four years since She Reads Truth began, I've logged dozens of hours in our pastor's study, praying and seeking counsel about how to walk in obedience and wise stewardship of a ministry the Lord created and called me to lead in the matter of a few short months. We met regularly to pray about the ministry, the heavy responsibility, and even my transition from stay-at-home mom to full-time ministry leader.

Our history in this building is rich and sweet. But the history of this stone structure goes back far before my family and I first stepped foot through its white double doors.

It goes back over a century to 1890, the year it was destroyed by fire and rebuilt for the third time. And back even further to the Civil War, when the pews and floors were damaged and the church records were burned. The history of this building goes back even beyond that, to 1849, the year it was first built by a Southern Baptist congregation. The very first men and women took their places—men on the left, women and children on the right—in the new wooden pews on a Sunday morning.

Just a few years ago, the original pulpit was discovered in storage and restored to use at the front of the sanctuary. It has two worn spots on top, one on each side, where generations of pastors gripped its edges, sensing the urgency and efficacy of the gospel they were preaching.

Over a century and a half later, Ryan and I would find ourselves seated in the very front pew, singing and reading Scripture about heaven at our own daughter's memorial service. In the years that followed we would worship through tearful, too-soon good-byes of friends' children, spouses, and parents, all punctuated by weddings, nursery duty, and choir rehearsals.

One hundred sixty-seven years. That's how long this stone church has stood. Decades and decades of families, births, deaths, congregants coming and going, pastors, Lord's Prayers, Apostles' Creeds, and Lord's Suppers. That's 8,684 sermons, not counting the seasons that required three services on Sunday mornings to accommodate the crowds. Over 60,000 days of existence, more permanent than the people or circumstances or joys or struggles that entered through its doors. Yet this building, in constant need of repair, reminds us that even the structure itself is temporary, as is most everything we hold dear.

This church stands as a reminder of both the impermanence of life and permanence of God.

WHAT IS PERMANENT?

The passing away that happens around and within us is real—you've seen a glimpse of that even in the stories we've shared in this book. But that which is permanent colors the temporary with hope and meaning. No longer is the passing away the primary reality. The overriding Truth is new, everlasting life in the gospel of Jesus.

So, exactly what is permanent?

Scripture tells us four things will last forever:

1. God is permanent.

In fact, He is uniquely eternal. In Revelation 1:8, God calls Himself the "Alpha and the Omega . . . who is, who was, and who is coming, the Almighty."

For I know that my Redeemer lives,
and at the last he will stand upon the earth. (Job 19:25 ESV)

Lord, you have been our dwelling place
in all generations.
Before the mountains were brought forth,
or ever you had formed the earth and the world,
from everlasting to everlasting you are God.
You return man to dust
and say, "Return, O children of man!"
For a thousand years in your sight
are but as yesterday when it is past,
or as a watch in the night. (Ps. 90:1–4 ESV)

In the beginning was the Word, and the Word was with God, and the Word was God. He was in the beginning with God. All things were made through him, and without him was not any thing made that was made. (John 1:1–3 ESV)

For in him all things were created: things in heaven and on earth, visible and invisible, whether thrones or powers or rulers or authorities; all things have been created through him and for him. (Col. 1:16 NIV)

2. God's Word is permanent.

Scripture was breathed out by God at specific times in history and is complete. It is reliable and true, a means for our souls to know and grow in relationship with our Creator.

Every word of God proves true;
he is a shield to those who take refuge in him. (Prov. 30:5 ESV)

The grass withers, the flower fades,
but the word of our God will stand forever. (Isa. 40:8 ESV)

All Scripture is breathed out by God and profitable for teaching, for reproof, for correction, and for training in righteousness, that the man of God may be complete, equipped for every good work. (2 Tim. 3:16–17 ESV)

For no prophecy was ever produced by the will of man, but men spoke from God as they were carried along by the Holy Spirit. (2 Pet. 1:21 ESV)

3. Our souls are permanent.

Because we are made in God's image, we are eternal beings. Even though our bodies as we know them are only temporary, we will have eternal, glorified bodies when we die. Our physical bodies have physical limitations, but even when we breathe our last, our souls will continue.

. . . I shall dwell in the house of the LORD forever. (Ps. 23:6 ESV)

. . . the dust returns to the earth as it was, and the spirit returns to God who gave it. (Eccl. 12:7 ESV)

"And do not fear those who kill the body but cannot kill the soul." (Matt. 10:28 ESV)

What is sown is perishable; what is raised is imperishable. . . . It is sown a natural body; it is raised a spiritual body. If there is a natural body, there is also a spiritual body. (1 Cor. 15:42, 44 ESV)

4. God's Church is permanent.

Though the Church as we understand it will one day come to an end, it will also continue in the new heaven and earth as the Church triumphant, the bride of Christ. A people from every race and ethnicity on Earth will be together as one before the throne giving God the worship He is due.

> After this I looked, and behold, a great multitude that no one could number, from every nation, from all tribes and peoples and languages, standing before the throne and before the Lamb, clothed in white robes, with palm branches in their hands, and crying out with a loud voice, "Salvation belongs to our God who sits on the throne, and to the Lamb!" (Rev. 7:9–10 ESV)

> Let us rejoice and exult
>   and give him the glory,
> for the marriage of the Lamb has come,
>   and his Bride has made herself ready;
> it was granted her to clothe herself
>   with fine linen, bright and pure. (Rev. 19:7–8 ESV)

Of the four permanent things, one is supreme. Colossians 1:17 says God "is before all things and by Him all things hold together." God created His Church, our spirits, and His Word, and each of them exists for His glory. Permanent though these things may be, He alone must be worshiped.

> Know that the LORD, he is God!
>   It is he who made us, and we are his;
>   we are his people, and the sheep of his pasture. (Ps. 100:3 ESV)

WHAT IS PASSING AWAY?

If only four things will last forever, does that mean everything else is temporary?

In short, yes. Most everything we know in this life is temporary—wealth and worry, marble countertops and iPhones, permanent markers and scars, heartache and hair loss. For better or worse, we can't take any of it with us.

Even the people whom we adore body and soul (our friends, parents, children), Scripture says their (and our) days are like grass. We bloom "like a flower of the field" but when the wind passes over us, we vanish (Ps. 103:15–16).

This is where it gets tricky and tender all at once.

Because the days of every person are numbered, we cannot hang our eternal hope on any human. But because the soul of every person is permanent, we cannot dismiss any human. Breath is temporary but life is valuable. Years are limited, but each life has an eternal weight to it. We can hope for people, but we cannot hope in people.

Just as my "normal" passed away with my parents' divorce, and Amanda watched as her financial and emotional stability slipped away with a growing family and a shrinking income, there is nothing temporary that we can place our hope in. Only God Himself.

But just when you are tempted to throw your hands up in futility, look again—this is good news! Nothing that is passing away can give us salvation anyway, and the One who can save us, can save us forever.

And the world is passing away along with its desires, but whoever does the will of God abides forever. (1 John 2:17 esv)

MANY TEMPORARY THINGS ARE GOOD

It seems incomplete to sort all of life into only two categories: "Permanent" and "Passing Away." Four things in one bucket, everything else in the other. If we are intended to care most deeply for the things in the permanent bucket, does that mean we should despise the contents of the temporary one? Do our friends and families really have to sit in the same category as yard clippings and obnoxious dance trends?

It's clear that not all temporary things are equal. In fact, there are many temporary things which God distinguishes as "good."

A study of the Scriptures, beginning with Creation, tells us that the earth itself and everything in it (water, plant life, and the animal kingdom) were designed and called "good" by God (Gen. 1:31). Even work, which existed before the fall when God set Adam to the task of tending the garden and naming the animals, was important and worth doing well (Gen. 2:15, 19–20). In fact, work is one of the ways we continue to bear God's image when we produce, create, and rest (Gen. 2:3; Eccl. 9:10).

Our bodies are good and they are important. The curse brought thistles and sweat to work and aches and defects to the body, but in spite of these limitations, God tells us our bodies are His temple and to be used for His glory (1 Cor. 3:16–17; 6:19–20).

Another "good" yet temporary thing is the function of the church as we know it. While the body of Christ is part of God's permanent, perfect plan, the functions we carry out on this earth are temporary. Even Christ's instruction to partake of communion, which we "do in remembrance" of Him (Luke 22:19), will only be needed "until He comes" again. (1 Cor. 11:26). The Lord's Supper will one day be fulfilled by the marriage supper of the Lamb (Rev. 19:6–9).

Think of all the beauty around us—art, food, music, and dance. These are things that awaken emotion in us, and they are good. Beauty allows us to express and to feel, and can even be a vehicle for worship. A friend of mine once told me that whenever he eats sushi, he thinks, "When God made rice, seaweed, soybeans, and fish, I wonder if He thought, 'When they figure out how to bring these things together, it is going to blow their minds.'"

Beauty and bodies, creation and the work of the local church—none of these are permanent, but all of them are good.

IDOL FACTORIES

If you filled a basket with the temporary, good things in your life, what would be in it? It would probably have your people in it—family and friends; it may have your work—how you feel called to spend your days; laughter over good food with the people you love; beautiful landscapes and sounds and smells. I imagine your basket is lovely, and that it contains things that are special just to you, that may not have any meaning for others. These are the things you love.

We know many of these things are good because God calls them good in His Word. And so, these things exist for God's glory and our enjoyment, but none of them is deserving of our worship. But because we live in a fallen world, we are often tempted to worship "something created instead of the Creator" (Rom. 1:25).

Are you ever tempted to worship your good things?

Is there anything in your basket that you just "can't live without"?

The good stuff is what the Tempter uses to draw our affections away from the Creator and onto the creation. We are tempted to care for, consider, and rely on the good thing more deeply than we care for, consider, and rely on God. That's all it takes for something to become an idol—our eternal souls placing their greatest affection on something that will turn to dust.

In his book *Counterfeit Gods*, Tim Keller calls the human heart an "idol factory that takes good things like a successful career, love, material possessions, even family, and turns them into ultimate things. Our hearts deify them as the center of our lives, because, we think, they can give us significance and security, safety and fulfillment, if we attain them."[1]

I remember watching the Super Bowl a few years ago with my sister and our families. We typically check in and out of the action, but we always give our full focus to the end when the winning team is wearing their embroidered "champion" hats and confetti floats endlessly from the sky. We love that part! That particular night, as we watched the MVP kiss the trophy and hoist it over his head, she said quietly, "This is exciting, but it's all ashes and dust, Rae. None of this will last." Then she asked me to pass the guacamole.

Now, it's only fair to acknowledge that my sister isn't much of a sports enthusiast to begin with, and if we had been talking about Strunk and White's *Elements of Style* or a pretty floral dress at Anthropologie, it may have been a little tougher for those words to roll off her tongue. Still, her wisdom stuck with me long after the confetti was indeed swept away. There is nothing innately wrong with sports, or climbs to the top of Everest, or master's degrees, or big beautiful homes, or even a really lovely pair of earrings. They only become idols when we turn a good thing into an ultimate thing.

It makes sense, but it sure does sting. My family is one of the most important things in my life. My kids are my own flesh and blood, and if we had adopted children, they would be just as fiercely ours. A lot of times, I am compelled to say "no" to good things because I've chosen to make my family a priority.

I wonder how many times I've chosen my family over God.

---

1. Tim Keller, *Counterfeit Gods: The Empty Promises of Money, Sex, and Power, and the Only Hope that Matters* (New York, NY: Penguin, 2011), xiv.

I wonder how often I've elevated the good work of pointing women to God's Word over actually opening and studying Scripture myself.

Sometimes, something important but temporary becomes more valuable to me than that which is permanent. Sometimes, we find ourselves holding tight to outdoor adventures or career milestones or teeth whitening, relying on them for our joy and fulfillment, and we stop holding tight to God.

ONE STABLE ROCK

Just one year after the stone chapel was constructed on the corner of Church and 3rd in Franklin, Tennessee, a man named Charles Haddon Spurgeon became a Christian and the pastor of another stone church in Southwark, London.

Both churches would be reminded quickly and often that their buildings and everything in them were passing away. But both the church in Tennessee and the one in Southwark would continue to gather and worship and study Scripture because they understood that no matter what was passing away, their souls were permanent and so was their God.

More than a century and a half separate us from when the stones and mortar were laid to build the little chapel, and the same amount of time separates us from the sermons and writings of Pastor Spurgeon. But God's Truth is timeless—it's permanent. And God often uses the words of men and women who walked with Him long before us to remind us just how permanent He is.

In his time as a minister, Spurgeon often wrote about the timelessness of God. He encouraged his congregation then, and us now, not to permit our hearts to cherish as ultimate, things that are passing away. Instead, we can find our satisfaction in Christ alone:

It is well there is one stable rock amidst the billows of the sea of life.

O my soul, set not thine affections upon rusting, moth-eaten, decaying treasures, but set thine heart upon Him who abides forever faithful to thee. Build not thine house upon the moving quicksands of a deceitful world, but found thy hopes upon this rock, which, amid descending rain and roaring floods, shall stand immovably secure.

My soul, I charge thee, lay up thy treasure in the only secure cabinet; store thy jewels where thou canst never lose them. Put thine all in Christ; set all thine affections on His person, all thy Hope in His merit, all thy trust in His efficacious blood, all they joy in His presence.[2]

Decaying treasures. It's not a very flattering way to think about our homes and husbands and handbags, is it? Spurgeon is praying that he would set his affections on God—the One who is truly, ever faithful. He charges himself (and us) to store our jewels where we can never lose them, but we know he's not saying there is such a place. He's suggesting we change what we consider to be our jewels.

THE PALMAR GRASP

We were created to hold tight.

If you've spent much time around newborns, you may have noticed that when you place your finger or a toy in their palm, they will involuntarily close their fingers around it. Amazingly, this grip can be tight

---

2. Charles Haddon Spurgeon, *Morning by Morning* (Peabody, MA: Hendrickson Publishing, 2006), 132.

enough for the baby to support its full body weight—though it's probably best for you to just take my word on that.

As early as eleven weeks in utero, and until they're about six months old, babies demonstrate a critical developmental reflex known as the Palmar Grasp.

Holding is as natural as breathing.

Even before we took our first breath, our fists have been naturally exercising the motion of grasping and holding. Well into adulthood we continue to employ that instinctual motion, and without it, our function would be deeply limited.

This Christmas we surprised our kids with a puppy under the tree. Not many weeks after that magical morning, I learned to tighten my grip on Lady's leash whenever she spots any feathered thing (a natural yet unforeseen consequence of inviting a bird dog into our home). Her body slows into that classic, pointing pose, and I know I'd better get ready.

I also hold tight when I play the "how few trips can I make between the house and the garage" game, making sure none of the grocery bag handles slip loose from my hands. It only takes one shattered-glass-and-syrup mess on the kitchen floor to want to prevent that from happening ever again.

I tighten my grip on the steering wheel when traffic is crazy on the interstate—especially when those show-off motorcyclists blast past on one wheel. There's nothing like the threat of involuntary manslaughter to keep your eyes on the road and hands square at "ten and two." (Or is it "nine and three" now?)

And whenever we visit our favorite city, I now habitually hold tight to my purse on the crowded Downtown Chicago streets. Lesson learned, you guys.

The truth is, real-world holding tight is often associated with anxiety or fear—we're trying to prevent something bad from happening.

We hold our people tight—holding hands as we cross the street, and supporting our grandparents as they proceed cautiously down a set of stairs.

Those grip marks on either side of the pulpit in my church? They were worn into the wood by decades of shepherds lovingly guiding their flocks away from danger and into safety.

Even when we hold tight out of affection, there is always still an element of fear—of not wanting to lose something. We want to protect our children from traffic, our grandma from falling, and the world from not knowing Jesus. Even impassioned "holding tight" is preventative in nature.

HE WON'T LET GO

We took our kids to Disney World for spring break this year.

Since we believe ourselves to be the "go big, just once" type of Disney-goers, rather than the "go briefly and often" type, we booked seven days of park-hopping magic, determined to experience every inch of every park at least twice. Ultimate Disney satisfaction. And, as it turns out, exhaustion.

Disney World is a crowded place. With the spring break crowds added to the mix, we quickly discovered another natural human reflex known as the "Disney Grasp." By hour six of day five, somewhere between Splash Mountain and Casey's Corner, Oliver registered a polite complaint, "Mom, I don't like the way you're holding my hand. It's just kind of straight and floppy—I need you to squeeze your fingers around mine."

This would have been a darling request in any other setting, but his hand was sweaty, and my fingers were tired and a little stiff from five days straight of hand holding (punctuated, of course, by the thrill of waving freely in the breeze on a fun roller-coaster ride for three minutes every three hours). Oliver wanted me to squeeze with meaning, and at that moment, all I really wanted was find a quiet place and not be touched or talked to for just a minute.

Of course, I complied. He didn't want to hold my limp-fish hand and I wanted him to feel secure. I would continue to forget his preferred squeeze level, however, and he would have to reach across his body and wrap my fingers back around his every hour or so for the rest of our trip. He knew my hand was tired, and I knew he wanted to be held tight, and so I thanked him for reminding me and readjusted my grip.

Parent-child relationships can be beautiful examples of how we relate with God. But when it comes to the realities of permanent and passing away, even the most enduring love of a parent cannot hold up. I love my son like crazy, and it is my job to keep him safe, but my hand eventually gives way. I get tired and I forget to hold him tight.

It's not that way with God.

Because everything in this world is fragile, there is no real-life metaphor for holding tight to something that is actually secure. We hold out of fear, we grip out of anxiety or prevention, and we eventually lose our grip every time. But because the gospel of Jesus Christ is permanent, it is not subject to the same shortcomings of anything that is passing away.

Hear that. The gospel is not passing away.

God does not let go.

The very nature of the gospel is different than anything else around us. Scripture calls our gospel inheritance "a living hope." Not a dying hope. The apostle Peter describes it as, "imperishable, undefiled, and unfading, kept in heaven for you." And the hope of the not-passing-away gospel is literally being "guarded" by God Himself (1 Pet. 1:3–5 ESV).

Guarded in heaven by God's own power. No wonder He tells us not to fear. No wonder He promises we can stake our lives on His Truth. This is why God told Abram, "Fear not, Abram: I am thy shield, and thy exceeding great reward" (Gen. 15:1 KJV). It's why the angel of the Lord said to

Mary, "Fear not, for behold, I bring you good news of great joy that will be for all the people" (Luke 2:10 ESV).

The gospel is good news. It is not scary news.

The gospel calls us to hold tight. But it also reminds us that we are already being held.

RELEASING THE BASKETS

I want you to picture something with me.

That basket of "good things" you imagined just a bit ago? The one with the people and places and work, the beautiful sights and smells and sounds that you love? It has a counterpart. You also have a basket of burdens that you carry with you wherever you go.

I carry worry in my basket—concern for my family and friends, and fear of regret or too much change. I have a handful of broken relationships in there too; some are my own doing, some theirs. Most are a combination of both. I've been betrayed, and my heart has been broken. That's in there, too. I carry my sin in that basket. I carried shame in there for a long time, too.

Picture yourself, struggling to juggle both burgeoning baskets. You're afraid to set down any of the good stuff, unsure how to hand over the rest. Some might suggest you hand both baskets to God, then stand alone, finally relieved of your burdens and missing your good things. I am not suggesting that. The gospel is so much better than that.

I do want you to place that basket of burdens in God's infinite, caring, gentle hands. It may take time, you may have to do it one item at a time, but with each transfer your relief becomes more evident and God proves Himself unwaveringly faithful.

You thought letting go of your burdens was tough, but when it comes to the basket of good things, it is exponentially more difficult to release them completely. Sure, you can trust your good things to God, but can you give them completely back to the One who gave them? Can you really let them be His and not yours? With reluctance or enthusiasm or somewhere very honest and in between, you release your tight grip and ask God to hold them for you.

But then.

You climb in with them, and you hold on tight. In the palm of that infinite, steadfast hand.

By holding tight to the Permanent Thing, you are trusting Him to hold on to all of the rest. And being held by Him, and holding Him tightest, you are trusting Him with your very life, and all of the blessings and burdens that come with it. You aren't holding them together—you are holding tight to Him alone, asking Him to carry the rest.

You are finally holding tight to Permanent in a world that's passing away.

THE GREATEST TREASURE

Just after the Civil War ended, at the same time Charles Spurgeon was pastoring a congregation in England, a husband and wife in Chicago, Illinois, came to understand what it would mean to find rest in God's permanence, even as their treasures were destroyed.

The family was wealthy; he was a successful lawyer with influential friends. They had four beautiful children—three girls and a boy—until scarlet fever stole the life of their only son. The boy was just four years old.

A year later, the man invested a sizeable portion of their money in Chicago's growing real estate market. Several months later, it was gone—the property and the family fortune destroyed by the Great Chicago Fire of 1871.

But what came next revealed what he treasured most.

The year was 1873, two years after the fire. They added another child to their family in that time, a total of four daughters. He sent his wife, Anna, and their children ahead to England for a family holiday. The man stayed back on business with the plan of following shortly after. Only, something went terribly wrong. The ship collided with another in the Atlantic, and the daughters perished at sea. A grieved Anna reached shore and sent her husband a telegram: "Survived alone."

When Horatio Spafford sailed past the very spot on the Atlantic where his four baby girls sank into the depths, he grieved the passing away of things he always knew were temporary. Then he offered up these words of worship to the God who never moved, who presides over all the sorrows and all the seas:

When peace, like a river, attendeth my way,
When sorrows like sea billows roll;
Whatever my lot, Thou has taught me to say,
It is well, it is well, with my soul.

Spafford penned the hymn "It Is Well with My Soul" at sea that day, weeping for what was lost, holding tight to what could never be lost.[3]

Maybe you've never felt the depth of that Job-like sorrow, but like me, you've probably stood stunned, in the wreckage of what was or what might have been. It's hard to imagine being able to "laugh at loss and defy destruction" as Spurgeon describes, or to think it could be truly "well" with our souls in the face of a tragedy like Spafford experienced.

But when we hold tight to Permanent, and trust Him to carry the rest, we really can count all else as loss, long before it is ever lost.

"But everything that was a gain to me, I have considered to be a loss because of Christ. More than that, I also consider everything to be a loss in view of the surpassing value of knowing Christ Jesus my

---

3. Derek W. H. Thomas, *Tabletalk* magazine, March 1, 2008.

Lord" (Phil. 3:7–8). Like Paul, we say this with much joy, even knowing the chains of trial we're sure to one day endure. Because those chains, though real and grievous, cannot bind the love and grace and mercies that are ours in Christ. When we hold tight to Permanent, knowing we are also held by Him, our greatest treasure is always safe.

SHE READS TRUTH

I PETER 1:3–9 ESV

Blessed be the God and Father of our Lord Jesus Christ! According to his great mercy, he has caused us to be born again to a living hope through the resurrection of Jesus Christ from the dead, to an inheritance that is imperishable, undefiled, and unfading, kept in heaven for you, who by God's power are being guarded through faith for a salvation ready to be revealed in the last time. In this you rejoice, though now for a little while, if necessary, you have been grieved by various trials, so that the tested genuineness of your faith—more precious than gold that perishes though it is tested by fire—may be found to result in praise and glory and honor at the revelation of Jesus Christ. Though you have not seen him, you love him. Though you do not now see him, you believe in him and rejoice with joy that is inexpressible and filled with glory, obtaining the outcome of your faith, the salvation of your souls.

SHE IS ME

Holding Tight to the Truth That Holds You

I am awake after a night of fitful sleep, haunted by the things I cannot control. The scenarios in my dreams are fictional and strange, but they conjure up feelings true and familiar. Too much weight on too-weak shoulders. Not enough time and insufficient trying.

Managing the chaos has become my habit; numbing the need is my survival mode of choice. There are days I'm convinced I'm succeeding, but not today. Today even the untrained eye could recognize the ruse.

On any given day I look to a short list of usual suspects for my identity. My phone and my laptop, my calendar and my lists—these false friends prey on my weakness while I blindly reach to them for strength. They never fail to fail me.

Today is different. Today I leave those false friends where they lie and resign myself to a breaking that is long overdue.

This moment has been coming and I've known it. It is no secret that I've been barely hanging on. But fighting to keep your grip is what you do when you feel like you're falling, no matter if you're falling down or falling short—especially if you're both.

It is time now and I'm ready, even relieved.

I take my worn Bible off the hotel desk and place it on the coffee table. I open the balcony door to let the salt air rush in, standing still for a long moment inside the sound of the waves. Raechel always tells me to travel with a tin candle and this is the first time I've listened, so I find the red book of matches and light the wick. I sit on the floor, take a deep breath, and open the thin, crackling pages.

I turn to an old favorite, 1 Corinthians 13. I must have read it one hundred times before.

> If I speak in the tongues of men and of angels, but have not love, I am a noisy gong or a clanging cymbal. And if I have prophetic powers, and understand all mysteries and all knowledge, and if I have all faith, so as to remove mountains, but have not love, I am nothing. If I give away all I have, and if I deliver up my body to be burned, but have not love, I gain nothing. (vv. 1–3 ESV)

Yes, yes. Love is the thing. Love conquers all, love casts out fear, love wins and all that. But if all I need is love, why am I so desperate for lesser things?

I want the language of angels—the right words for my lips and my pen, the right actions to hold them up and follow them through. I long to understand these mysteries, to have knowledge and faith—oh, how I need faith! I desire the selflessness that gives without keeping a record of cost—to rid myself of this self-absorption that shocks me with its demands and threatens to hurt the people I love.

If I muster up love, can't I have these others too? I wish the apostle Paul were here so I could ask him. Instead, I read on from verse 4:

> Love is patient and kind; love does not envy or boast; it is not arrogant or rude. It does not insist on its own way; it is not irritable or resentful; it does not rejoice at wrongdoing, but rejoices with the truth. Love bears all things, believes all things, hopes all things, endures all things. (vv. 4–7 ESV)

Yes! Again, yes. This love is the goal. This is the love that is of Christ. It's the kind of love proclaimed from the pulpit of elaborate weddings, the kind we sing songs about as children. This is the love that turns all that clanging noise into an effortless symphony. Surely I can remember it this time around. Surely I can get it right if I try hard enough.

With another deep breath, I look down at verse 8:

> Love never ends.

I pause, shifting uncomfortably where I sit, legs crossed under the glass tabletop. They look like triangle appliques on the geometric lines of the hotel carpet. I study the design for a moment, preparing for what I know is next.

> As for prophecies, they will pass away; as for tongues, they will cease; as for knowledge, it will pass away. For we know in part and we prophesy in part, but when the perfect comes, the partial will pass away. (vv. 8–10 ESV)

"When the perfect comes, the partial will pass away." I read the sentence again slowly. Perfect. Partial. My head and shoulders drop low at the weight of the words. Which one did I wake up today hoping to find? Did I long for one and reach for the other?

The black letters begin to swirl on the page as tears flood into my eyes, and I shut them tight because I know. I know once again what I've forgotten ten thousand times over. I know what I need and what I'm really looking for.

It's Jesus. Even when I don't know it, I'm looking for Jesus.

I'm opening God's Word to find the Living Word—the One "who was with God in the beginning," the Word who "became flesh and took up residence among us" (John 1:2, 14).

The tears come quietly and I go ahead and let them, wet eyes focusing in on verse 11:

> When I was a child, I spoke like a child, I thought like a child, I reasoned like a child. When I became a man, I gave up child-ish ways. (1 Cor. 13:11 ESV)

This is the moment when I sense Him lifting up my head and gently redirecting my gaze—up from my need, up from my circumstances, up from my narrow reality—to see them in the fullness of His glory. My loving Father coaxes my eyes up to the story—His story—happening all around me. I have been earnestly focused on a single star, while He patiently gestures to the galaxy.

> For now we see in a mirror dimly, but then face to face. Now I know in part; then I shall know fully, even as I have been fully known. (v. 12 ESV)

Oh, how dim is this mirror before me! *But God.* He is the God who penned redemption's story, from before the beginning of time all the way to the fingertips of eternity's outstretched hand. He is the God who is not bound by my efforts nor held back by my doubt. He is the God who is

Love infinite, Love perfected, Love inextinguishable. He is the greatest of these.

> So now faith, hope, and love abide, these three; but the great-
> est of these is love. (v. 13 ESV)

His faithfulness is shattering my illusion of self-sufficiency in this moment, busting the myth of my fix-it faith, and bringing me back to the Truth, the gospel of grace.

The silent tears have now become sobs, but I don't give a thought to who might hear my cries through the open balcony door. All that matters is that I've found Him. Or rather, He has found me.

I came to the Book for knowledge, but here I find that I am fully known.

I came looking for faith, hope, love, but here I encounter Love Himself.

I came shortsighted—looking for the temporary, the partial—but I find myself looking into the beautiful, unmatched face of the Perfect.

HOLD ON

That was me.

That was me, being drawn back to the merciful face of my compassionate God after looking for comfort in my effort and my plans.

That was me, opening God's Word to find Him after days and weeks of opening it out of obligation.

That was me, broken at the realization that He was still there, holding me, even when I'd loosened my grip on Him.

Before you leave these pages, heart beating with a renewed resolve to hold tight to the Permanent Things, it is important that you know this: Raechel and I have not magically become better versions of the women you read about in these pages. There's no spectrum from broken to holy; but if there were, we'd be firmly planted at one end.

We are forgetful, needing constant reminders of who we are and who He is.

We are doubters, desperate for Him to fill us with faith.

We are sinners, requiring His grace to forgive our trespasses and heal the wounds they cause.

We are weak, utterly hopeless without His strength.

And that's exactly the point, dear friends. Truth is for us—even for us.

God's promises, covenant, love, mercy, hope, sovereignty—His gospel—is for the likes of us. We who hold on to all the wrong things are held tight by the love of the unchanging, unfading, one true God.

We don't hold tight because we've figured this out. We hold tight because He holds us.

Raechel and I have a running joke that only one of us is allowed to break down at a time. Operating a ministry together is a lot like a marriage. You're in this, for better or for worse, and all the tedium, nuance, surprises, and tension in between.

Sometimes the in-between takes its toll, and we . . . well, we lose our minds a little. But it works out okay because we have each other. Like an old couple sitting in their recliners across the living room from one another, we look up from our work from time to time to make sure the other is doing okay. We've learned to recognize each other's signs of distress, and when one of us is at our lowest, the other tags in with a chorus of, "You've got this, buddy," "Let's go for a walk," or, our favorite, "We're gonna make it."

Our ups and downs have taken the form of an unintentionally well-choreographed dance, and we've learned to trust that when one partner is all but ready to quit, the other will carry her along. The timing is undeniably providential, but there have been a few close calls. The day of my hotel-room breakdown was one of those.

We were a couple states away from home for a women's conference at which we would speak the next day. We're not speakers by trade but there are times God has put us on a stage anyway, and out of obedience (and probably a smidge of pride, if we're honest), we go.

In different rooms of the same hotel, we sat, I with my Bible and she with hers. We were both breaking. We were both grasping. And, by no plan of our own, we were both reading 1 Corinthians 13.

After that reckoning I had with the Lord in the pages of His Word—the one where He convicted my heart for the umpteenth time of coming to Scripture for a quick fix instead of a slow and deep relationship with Him—I washed my face, gathered my wits, and went down to the patio to meet Raechel for lunch.

We sat facing the ocean, quietly discussing the weekend's schedule—where we needed to be at what times, what we would say, what we would wear. But what we were really, separately wondering was, *What in the world are we doing here?* Raechel showed her cards first.

She looked up at me over our hotel hamburgers with tears in her eyes, and said two words: "I can't."

My initial reaction was to kick into partner fix-it gear. "Sure you can. *We* can. And also, well, we have to. But it'll be okay, really!" She wasn't buying it. I wasn't either. That's when my tears followed.

"I know," I said. "I can't either."

And so we cried. And we prayed. And right there in that hotel restaurant, we opened the Book we spend our days telling women around the world to open. And it was still true.

God's Word was true, even though everything in us doubted. God's Word was true, even though part of us didn't want to believe it. God's Word was true, even though every engine in ourselves seemed to be firing with shame, accusation, hopelessness, and fear. The Truth was still true.

Sometimes holding tight will feel more like hanging on, but don't give up. Don't believe the lie that you should let go. God holds you. Hold tight to Him.

THIRSTY

We're beverage people.

The refrigerator at the She Reads Truth office is filled with all manner of choices—Sprite, LaCroix, Diet Coke, water. There are coffee options and tea options and sometimes homemade infused-water options. Food and drink is our love language, and we speak it often.

All day long, the cups appear. In the conference room, on desks and coffee tables—any surface is fair game.

Lunchtime is our favorite time, and everyone in the office knows it. It's an event, usually. First, there's the long discussion about where we'll eat. That usually starts around 10:55 a.m. Then orders are placed around 11:30, and the eating commences at noon. We sit around the conference room table, with our plates and takeout containers and cups, and we talk—but not about work. We talk about our favorite and least favorite things, we talk about what we were like as kids, we talk about the last time we went to the movies or that long-lost album we can't get enough of. We ask about most embarrassing moments and which animals are the best pets.

Sometimes, when the laughter has faded into sounds of contented chomping, we talk about what's in our cups. Not LaCroix, or water, or green tea lemonade—but the things that we're worried about, or hoping for, or wishing we could go back and fix.

We each have a cup, and it's always full of something.

You'd be surprised how easy it is to forget. We spend our workdays with Truth—reading it and writing about it, giving it a beautiful home in books and online, making sure everyone within earshot knows they're invited into its pages. Sometimes we forget to stop. We forget to look at the person working next to us and say, *I see you there. Truth is for you, too.*

In an office of full cups and open Bibles, we can still walk around thirsty.

Holding tight to Truth is a little like drinking. It's God who provides the water and gives us the ability to take it in, but we still have to hold it to our lips and drink.

WHEN YOU CAN'T

A lot of crying happened that weekend at the beach. Raechel and I left the hotel two days later, feet still squarely in the "I can't do it" camp. But the Holy Spirit's nudge wouldn't let up, and we wanted to listen. We wanted to trust Him and obey, together.

At a gate 2 in the tiny Daytona Beach airport, against our better human judgment, we asked God to remove all our excuses. Then we boarded a plane for home.

When the flight landed, we emerged from different sections of the plane, the beginnings of a book introduction in my hand and an outline in hers. When we compared notes, we knew—they belonged to the same book. They belonged to *this* book.

Writing this book was the thing we couldn't do.

Writing this book was also the thing we couldn't *not* do.

The significance of that story has nothing to do with me, and it has nothing to do with Raechel. It has nothing to do with gumption or stick-to-it-ness, or about our desire to follow the Lord's leading. What I'm telling you is about the weakness of those things. Our gumption was long gone. Our desire to follow the Lord was waning. God was the faithful one.

God *is* the faithful one.

This book is not a directive to make your life better by reading your Bible every day. This book is evidence that He gives life to dead things through the power of His Word. Not once, not occasionally, but currently and all the time.

Our Savior does more than fill in the gaping holes of our brokenness. Our sovereign Lord does more than pick us up where we fall short. Our holy God holds all things together. He holds us together. His Word is not something we add to our life to get us from dawn to dusk. His Word is Life.

Friends, our earnest prayer is that you set this book aside and hold tight to the only Book that will last. Truth stands, without us. It does not need our vote of confidence or our help. It certainly doesn't need our words or our carefully-crafted metaphors. Truth stands and it will stand, period.

God's promises are permanent when the world's promises pass away.

God's covenant is permanent when our good intentions pass away.

God's love is permanent when our good behavior passes away.

God's mercy is permanent when our bodies pass away.

God's hope is permanent when our plans are passing away.

God's sovereignty is permanent when our power is passing away.

The gospel is permanent when our belief is passing away.

The permanent is there for you. Whatever this temporary life has looked like, and whatever signs are waiting on the road ahead, God and His Truth will always be true.

You cannot change the Truth. You cannot earn it or lose it or escape it. But you can hold on to it, knowing that it holds you.

SHE READS TRUTH

ROMANS 8:31-39

THE BELIEVER'S TRIUMPH

What then are we to say about these things?
If God is for us, who is against us?

He did not even spare His own Son
but offered Him up for us all;
how will He not also with Him grant us everything?

Who can bring an accusation against God's elect?
God is the One who justifies.
Who is the one who condemns?

Christ Jesus is the One who died,
but even more, has been raised;
He also is at the right hand of God
and intercedes for us.

Who can separate us from the love of Christ?
Can affliction or anguish or persecution
or famine or nakedness or danger or sword?

As it is written:
Because of You
we are being put to death all day long;
we are counted as sheep to be slaughtered.

No, in all these things we are more than victorious
through Him who loved us.
For I am persuaded that not even death or life,
angels or rulers,
things present or things to come, hostile powers,
height or depth, or any other created thing
will have the power to separate us
from the love of God that is in Christ Jesus our Lord!

ACKNOWLEDGMENTS

RAECHEL

When you write a book about your life, you are rarely the only character in the story. There are other players. Other people who saw you when you felt unseen, heard you when you felt unheard. People who prayed grace over the little girl with the odds stacked against her. There is the cast of players that make these stories what they are. The temporary people God used to remind me that Permanent exists. To them I am grateful.

To Mom, especially, and to Rebecca. To Ryan for being a safe place to feel scared. To Oliver, Hazel, and our beloved Evie Grace. To Roger and Bev, Greg and Gary, to Uncle Dave and Aunt Annette, and to Grandma Marvolene. To Bill the bus driver and Kathy Heck. To Katie Creech and the Parish/Cornerstone women who pointed me to God's Truth—who reminded me it hadn't changed, even when I couldn't read it for myself. To Kaitlin for keeping me straight. To Jessi and Kacia and Maggie— three of the very first Shes. To George and Karen and to Nate and the many others I could go on listing. All of these are passing away, but they are some of the sweetest breaths that will pass over this earth.

After the cast of people who play in the stories, comes the crowd of people who help us craft them. To Bryan Norman, especially, and to Jennifer Lyell. To the entire team at B&H and LifeWay, and to the team of praying, cheering, editing, double-checking girls at #SRThq. To Ally Fallon, Amanda Barnhart, and Ryan (again) for their encouragement and effort to produce beautiful words.

To Amanda Bible Williams. For teaching me what it feels like to genuinely miss a person when they're gone. Thank you.

And to the Permanent One, who has never failed, never changed, never passed away—who holds tight to everything so I don't have to. Great is Your faithfulness.

AMANDA

I am one person who put some words on a page. But this book is a product of so much more than that. Here are just a handful of the people who held up my arms, not only in the writing of this book, but through the joy and sorrow of living my page of God's great story. I owe them a lifetime of thanks.

To my mom, the most permanent figure in my temporary life. There is not a book big enough to hold my gratitude and love for you. To my dad. I wish you were here to read these words of how your life changed mine. I thank God you are part of my story.

To David, for teaching me how to be loved. And to our three children, who tire me and inspire me to no end. I love you always and forever, no matter what.

To Jamey, for always cheering me on. To Aunt Wanda, for loving me and mine so well. To J. Wayne and Susan, for raising my favorite human and treating me like your own. To Shane, Trish, and Jennifer, for your love and support across years and miles.

To Fran, Erin, Kristel, Michelle, Mindy, Dara Lynn, Alexis, Rebecca, Kara, Suzanne, Duane, Lisa, and Leigh. Much of what I know about church, I've learned from you. To Kelley, Annie, and Ellie, for telling the truth and writing it down. Thank you all for being my people.

To Kaitlin, Ryan, Rebecca, Amanda, Russ, and the entire She Reads Truth team. You deserve all the gold stars. To Nate Shurden and Jim and Kim Thomas for your invaluable counsel. To Ally Fallon for helping make our map.

To Jennifer Lyell and the talented and patient teams at B&H and LifeWay. It is an honor to hold up Truth with you. To Bryan Norman. You are a stellar agent and an irreplaceable friend. Thank you for both.

To Raechel, for showing me what it means to lead and love at the same time. There's nobody like you.

Above all, to God the Father, who was and is and is to come. To You be all glory, now and forever, through Jesus Christ our Lord. Amen.

ABOUT THE AUTHORS

RAECHEL MYERS is always on the lookout for beauty, goodness, and truth in everyday life. Co-founder and CEO of She Reads Truth, Raechel has a bachelor's degree in housing and environmental design, and is not afraid to paint a whole house over a long weekend. She longs to cook artisanal meals, but loves Chinese takeout. She lives south of Nashville, Tennessee, with her three favorite people.

AMANDA BIBLE WILLIAMS likes words and books more than just about anything. She holds bachelor's degrees in psychology and English, nearly a master's in religion, and a deep love for a farmhouse east of Nashville, Tennessee, where she lives with her husband and their three children. Chief Content Officer of She Reads Truth, Amanda spends her days happily rearranging sentences and explaining that her maiden name really is Bible.

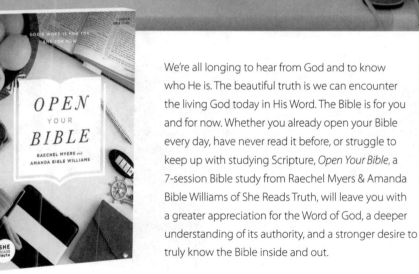

SHE READS TRUTH

Want more beauty, goodness, and Truth in your life? Join the She Reads Truth community.

Every day we read Scripture together—working our way through books of the Bible, topics that matter, and seasons of the Church calendar. We engage with God's Word and with each other. And we keep coming back, on the hard days and the good days, because God and His Word never change, regardless of our circumstances.

WE INVITE YOU TO JOIN US
AT SHEREADSTRUTH.COM OR ON
THE SHE READS TRUTH APP

@SHEREADSTRUTH